THE TASTE OF OUR TIME

Collection planned and directed by

ALBERT SKIRA

BIOGRAPHICAL AND CRITICAL STUDY

BY

PIERRE DUFOUR

Translated by Robert Allen

PICASSO 1950-1968

Color plate on the title page:
Bacchanal, November 25, 1959. Linocut.

★

Distributed in the United States by
THE WORLD PUBLISHING COMPANY
2231 West 110th Street, Cleveland, Ohio 44102

★

*T*his book picks up the story of Picasso's œuvre where my dear friend Maurice Raynal left off when he died. Pierre Dufour, who belongs to a much younger generation, observes that œuvre from a different angle and his conclusions cannot be measured with the same yardstick as those reached by Raynal. The latter wrote as a friend of the painter's and an eyewitness of the events he described. Dufour sees Picasso with a fresh eye—a very good thing, too. Many of the people who have written about him—and indeed about Juan Gris as well—have let themselves be hypnotized by a single period, what is called the heroic period of Cubism, and have judged the remainder of his œuvre only in relation to it. That period was undoubtedly of great, even decisive importance but we must not overlook the fact that the tool it forged was subsequently utilized for very different purposes.

At the start the Cubist painters were faced with the work of their elders, all of whom (except Cézanne), or so they thought, set more store on the content of a picture than on what Juan Gris called its "architecture," which in their own eyes was what counted most. On the other hand, photography had freed painting from the fetters of servile imitation, of illusionism. Their experiments led to the invention of a handwriting which, while safeguarding the structure of the picture as an object, enabled them to represent the world around them without imitating it. That, I think, is the crucial point to which we must always revert if we want to obtain a clear view not only of what Picasso and his friends undertook, but of contemporary art in general. A great many so-called "artists," by their inability to read at first sight and understand a non-imitative handwriting, showed themselves to be not painters or sculptors *but mere craftsmen. That they developed a non-figurative art which is termed "abstract" proves simply that they took the appearance for the substance of the work "read." They went astray, no less than those who, like some of the Surrealists, relapsed into an academic, abjectly imitative handwriting.*

Picasso, instead, has made free with the handwriting he himself invented and thus constantly enriched it. This has enabled him to unburden his soul more and more. His art has always been autobiographical and has grown increasingly so with advancing age. Today we can observe an extremely odd development—narrative art. As he said to me not long ago, "After all, a picture that tells a story is not such a bad thing." An art of this type is poles apart from an "abstraction" that does not want to represent anything and whose products are therefore but empty decorations which remain confined to the wall instead of blossoming out in the conscience of the spectator. For a veritable work of art can only be engendered with the collaboration of the spectator who observes it. I may be wrong, but it seems to me that a revival of narrative painting is taking place at the present time. Needless to say, it will owe nothing to the anecdotic painters of the nineteenth century.

One cannot insist enough on the spontaneity of Picasso's art, which is not the product of preconceived ideas and does not tend towards a pre-established goal. Picasso lives only in the present; he knows no past and thinks not of the future. For him a new world is born every morning. It is his real life and his dreams, his joys and his sorrows, his reactions and his obsessions, that he sets down and passes on to us. His development is not linear because it is linked with his life, which like all life is multiform.

It seems to me that Pierre Dufour has grasped this perfectly. The way in which he explains Picasso's progress in recent years, by analysing his most outstanding works, pinpoints his untrammelled freedom. For that reason I think this study can give an accurate picture of the great painter, a picture which is different from, and more exact than, those drawn in many other books on Picasso.

Daniel Henry Kahnweiler

CHRONOLOGICAL SURVEY

1949 **Birth of Paloma, Picasso's fourth daughter.**
Picasso paints the "Dove" for the poster of the World Peace Congress in Paris.
Works produced during the last four years on show in the Maison de la Pensée Française, Paris.

Matisse begins decorating the Chapelle du Rosaire at Vence.
Le Corbusier takes in hand the construction of an apartment block at Marseilles.

1950 **Picasso receives the freedom of Vallauris. Goes to England for the World Peace Congress.**
Produces "The Goat."

Exhibition of the Fauves at the 25th Venice Biennale (Braque, Derain, Van Dongen, Dufy, Friesz, Manguin, Matisse, Vlaminck, Valtat) and of "Four Masters of Cubism" (Braque, Gris, Léger, Picasso). Henri Matisse is awarded the prize for painting and Alexander Calder that for sculpture.

1951 **Picasso paints "Massacre in Korea."**
In Paris, he takes up his abode in an apartment in the Rue Gay-Lussac but keeps his studio in the Rue des Grands-Augustins.
Trip to Italy for the World Peace Congress.
Exhibition of sculpture in the Maison de la Pensée Française, Paris.
One-man shows in Tokyo (paintings, drawings, lithographs, ceramics) and in the Institute of Contemporary Art, London (drawings and lithographs since 1893).

Le Corbusier drafts the town plan for Chandigarh (Punjab).

1952 **Paints "War" and "Peace," huge compositions measuring 15½ by 33½ feet, set up one after the other in an abandoned chapel at Vallauris now called the Temple of Peace.**

M. Breuer, P. L. Nervi and B. H. Zehrfuss draft the plans for the UNESCO building in Paris (advisers L. Costa, W. Gropius, Le Corbusier, S. Markelius, E. N. Rogers, E. Saarinen), which is completed in 1957. Picasso, Arp, Moore, Calder, Miró, Afro, Appel, Tamayo, Matta and Artigas contribute to its decoration.
Death of Paul Eluard.

1953 **A year of great international exhibitions dedicated to Picasso. Retrospectives held in Lyons, Rome and Milan.**
Luciano Emmer makes a film about Picasso.
Picasso does the stage sets for Garcia Lorca's "Funeral Song of Ignacio Sanchez Mejias."
Breaks with Françoise Gilot.

Le Corbusier finishes building the chapel of Notre-Dame-du-Haut at Ronchamp he had commenced in 1950.

1954 **In spring, Picasso paints the series of portraits of Sylvette (Mlle D.). In summer, stays at Collioure and Perpignan. Jacqueline Roque becomes his companion.**
Exhibition in the Museum of Modern Art, São Paulo.

Braque and Léger exhibit their graphic work at the 27th Venice Biennale. Max Ernst awarded prize for painting; Jean Arp for sculpture; Miró for engraving.
Death of Matisse and of Maurice Raynal.

1955 **Picasso's wife, Olga Khoklova, dies early in the year at Cannes.**
In February he brings to a close the series of fifteen paintings inspired by Delacroix's "Women of Algiers" that he commenced on December 13 of the previous year.
Buys Villa "La Californie" near Cannes.
Clouzot makes the film entitled "The Picasso Mystery."
One-man shows in Paris (Musée des Arts Décoratifs) and Munich (Haus der Kunst).

Documenta I exhibitions at Kassel.
Death of Fernand Léger.

1956 **"Guernica" shown with the seventy preliminary studies and the variants in the Palais des Beaux-Arts, Brussels, in May and June, and in the Stedelijk Museum, Amsterdam, from July to September.**
Exhibitions in Cologne (Rheinisches Museum) and Hamburg (Kunsthalle).

1957 Starts work on the series of paintings inspired by Velazquez's "Las Meninas."
Great retrospective exhibition for Picasso's 75th birthday in the Museum of Modern Art, New York, and the Art Institute of Chicago.
Roland Penrose publishes "Portrait of Picasso."
Exhibition of graphic work in the Nationalgalerie, Berlin.

Death of Constantin Brancusi.
"Europa 1907" exhibition in the Stedelijk Museum, Amsterdam.

1958 February, Picasso paints "The Fall of Icarus" for the UNESCO building in Paris.
Marries Jacqueline Roque.
In autumn buys the Château de Vauvenargues on the slopes of Mont Sainte-Victoire near Aix-en-Provence.
Exhibition in the Museum of Fine Arts, Philadelphia.

Braque exhibition at the Venice Biennale.
"Renaissance of the 20th Century" exhibition in the Stedelijk Museum, Amsterdam.

1959 Picasso exhibitions in the Musée Cantini, Marseilles, and the Galerie Louise Leiris, Paris. The sculpture group entitled "The Bathers" shown in the Documenta II exhibition, Kassel.

Le Corbusier builds the Museum of Modern Art, Tokyo, and the monastery of Sainte-Marie-de-la-Tourette at Eveux, near Lyons.
Inauguration of the Guggenheim Museum, New York, designed by Frank Lloyd Wright.
Documenta II exhibitions at Kassel.

1960 The Arts Council of Great Britain organizes an exhibition of 269 works by Picasso in the Tate Gallery, London.
He works on the series of paintings and drawings inspired by Manet's "Déjeuner sur l'Herbe."

The Musée Fernand Léger opened at Biot.

1961 Picasso settles at Notre-Dame-de-Vie, Mougins (Riviera).
His 80th birthday is an occasion for celebrations all over the world and in particular at Vallauris.
Exhibition at the University of California Art Gallery, Los Angeles.

1962 Several exhibitions in New York under the title "Picasso: an American Tribute."
Exhibitions in the Galerie Louise Leiris, Paris.

9

1963 **Exhibition in the Galerie Rosengart, Lucerne.**

Death of Braque, Villon and Tzara.
"Idole und Dämonen" exhibition in the Museum of the 20th
Century, Vienna.

1964 **Exhibitions at Montreal and Toronto.**
Exhibitions in Japan (Tokyo, Kyoto and Nagoya).

32nd Venice Biennale: "Today's Art in the Museums" exhibition
(the Kunsthalle in Hamburg, the Nationalgalerie in Berlin and the
Musée National d'Art Moderne in Paris contributed one work by
Picasso each).

1965 **Exhibition in the Musée des Augustins, Toulouse, entitled:**
"Picasso et le Théâtre."

Death of Le Corbusier.

1966 **The whole world celebrates Picasso's 85th birthday.**
Exhibition in the Helena Rubenstein Pavilion, Tel Aviv.
The huge exhibition (508 works) entitled "Hommage à Picasso"
opened in the Grand Palais, Paris at the end of the year.

Death of André Breton, Jean Arp, Amédée Ozenfant and Alberto
Giacometti. "Dix Ans d'Art Vivant" exhibition in the Fondation
Maeght, Saint-Paul-de-Vence.

1967 **Exhibitions of drawings, pastels and watercolors at Fort Worth**
(Art Center Museum) and Dallas (Museum of Fine Arts).
Important exhibition in London (Tate Gallery) and New York
(Museum of Modern Art).

Death of Zadkine.

1968 **Exhibitions in the Galerie Louise Leiris, Paris (drawings done**
during the last three years).
Picasso continues to work at Notre-Dame-de-Vie, Mougins.

Documenta III exhibitions at Kassel.
Bauhaus exhibition at Stuttgart.
Death of Marcel Duchamp, Van Dongen and Foujita.

PICASSO TODAY

We must not let ourselves be taken in by the success of great contemporary painters: though famous, they are misunderstood.

D. H. KAHNWEILER

THE seventeenth century invented the church/art-gallery, the cathedral/museum; the twentieth has invented the museum/cathedral, the exhibition/rite, the retrospective show, the homage. The "Homage to Picasso" exhibition in Paris (1966-1967) was visited by nearly a million people in the few months it was open. In 1944, some of the Picasso canvases shown in the first Salon d'Automne held after the Liberation of Paris had been attacked and damaged. At the commemorative exhibition of 1966-1967, a sarcastic comment, even a smile, would have been out of place. Duly informed by newspapers, magazines and art books, the public diligently and docilely endeavored to recognize periods and styles, to identify Fernande, Dora Maar, Marie-Thérèse and Jacqueline. Subversive art was "rehabilitated" under the inoffensive form of a cult or a culture. Perusal of the catalogue enabled every visitor to become a historian. However, except for the blue and rose periods and the Ingresque phases, as one followed Picasso's path amongst the crowd that thronged the Grand Palais, one could not help thinking of one of his terrible sayings: "They'll find that bad anyway, and even if they find it good you may be sure that it will not be because of the painting."

What is Picasso today? He is still the myth of yesterday, a masker with various faces. The bohemian artist of the Bateau-Lavoir, the Cubist of the "heroic years," the stage designer of the Ballets Russes; the painter of Guernica, eternal exile from an ideal Spain, and the creator of the Dove of the Congress for Peace in the international aura of the immediate post-war period; the eagle-eyed, ironical craftsman, sculptor at Boisgeloup, lithographer at Mourlot's, potter at Vallauris; and the "old man crazy for painting" in the solitude of Notre-Dame-de-Vie, who sums up the lot; all these add up to the paradoxical, highly contrasted image now familiar to the whole world. Familiar yet enigmatic. From Montmartre to Mougins, from Fernande to Jacqueline: what a godsend for a certain type of literature is a life that seemingly writes itself entirely with the names of places and women. At the "digest" level the artist's oeuvre is merely the setting for his love life, the backdrop for a mythological play. And, far from bringing us down to reality, the economic phenomena of the present-day art market enhance the anaesthetizing action of the myth; one becomes permanently conditioned to unreality. "People don't buy my pictures," says Picasso. "They buy my signature."

Today Picasso is eighty-seven years old. Like Rembrandt, Goya and Renoir, he seems to ignore age in his artistic production and defy it with his amazing diversity and unquenchable vitality. What fascinates us in the work he has produced during the last twenty years is not only the variety of the media employed —painting, sculpture, drawing, engraving, pottery—but also the increasing subtlety of the accents and levels of expression. In addition to the intimate narrative of his "autobiography"— La Californie, Vauvenargues, Notre-Dame-de-Vie—and the frescoes of his "lofty sentiments"—*Massacre in Korea, The Temple of Peace, The Fall of Icarus*—we now find the dialogue with the masters of the past, El Greco, Delacroix, Velazquez, Manet. In *The Women of Algiers, Las Meninas,* the *Déjeuner sur l'Herbe,* did Picasso aim merely to test certain aspects of his art? Or did he want to pay a museum that for him is anything but "imaginary" the ambiguous tribute of a terroristic archaeology? When in other works he offers us variants of already known phases or subtle innovations, should we take it that he is simply "having a little fun," as some critics have assured us? Or is he merely continuing to employ his exceptionally keen plastic sense? Once again his work raises questions that are both multiple and essential.

These questions are topical too. At the very time when contemporary art hesitates whether to capitulate before the engineer-architect or seek escape in neo-Surrealist or neo-abstract solutions, Picasso—obstinately figurative and humanist in his own way when it seems that no one else is any longer—takes his stand once again in opposition. Not so long ago people could not understand the revolutionary artist. Today they are surprised that he does not, like so many others, settle down to imitate himself. "Imitate oneself, how contemptible!... One becomes one's own admirer. I don't sell myself anything."

A BREAK-AWAY ART

A picture is not a duplicate of reality, it is a sign.

PIERRE FRANCASTEL

THE misunderstandings between Picasso's art and the public are less far-fetched than is generally believed. Pierre Francastel in his study on the Italian Renaissance and, more recently, Pierre Charpentrat in his *Mirage baroque* (Baroque Mirage) have called attention to the ambiguity of arts that have become historical and the many misunderstandings to which they have given rise. This is virtually a general rule where the visual arts are concerned. As Maurice Jardot said, "The reading of the subject has been accomplished, the 'handwriting' of the work has nearly always remained undeciphered."

If the phenomenon is particularly noticeable in the case of Picasso and of modern art in general, it is because now that the anecdote has disappeared the spectator is called upon to read "the painting."

"Painting is stronger than I am," says Picasso, "it makes me do what it wants." If we take this for a witticism, it is because we are still tempted to use the conventions of yesterday to read the works of today. Until recently a painter was looked upon as a man who was able to reproduce or imagine a *spectacle*. It has often been said that since Cubism painting is less interested in representing a certain reality than in inventing a new reality on the canvas, yet we still view Cubist works as rather daring, rather baffling variants of the traditional image. But as a matter of fact the reference to reality in the Cubist *work-object* is subjected to such far-reaching transpositions that, immediately after the Cézannesque phase, it apparently made a radical break with the past. Thanks to Picasso, visual art has accomplished its revolution. Have the public and the critics accomplished theirs? There is some doubt about that.

Picasso himself has said: "The fact that for a long time Cubism was not understood, and that even today there are people who are unable to 'see' it, is of no importance. I cannot read English... That doesn't mean there is no such thing as the English language."

The misunderstanding was to be expected, for it was a question of nothing less than wiping out five centuries of western painting. Before the industrial image arrived on the scene—photographic, cinematographic, sound-tracked—Painting either displayed a colossal, permanent social decor on the walls of churches and palaces or, reduced to the scale of the easel, composed small-sized projections of genre scenes and landscapes for the enjoyment of the individual. But, whether celebration or escape, its function was always that of a spectacle. In painting art was closely linked with a phenomenon that is neither specifically nor necessarily aesthetic: the image. If Cubism succeeded in becoming something more than an episode in the history of taste and an improvement on Cézannism—which is what some people have tried to make it—that is because it denounced the century-long collusion between art and image. An image which, in all the periods when culture was highly intellectualized—Greco-Roman art, the Italian Renaissance, Classicism, Romanticism, Impressionism—has always been characterized by a realistic imitation that is the almost inevitable consequence of technical perfection.

Another factor that contributed to the power of the arts of the image was that their realism went hand in hand with hedonism, whereas Cubism dared to make a double break with imitation and with pleasantness.

"You are well aware," said Picasso to Kahnweiler in 1946, "why we started out with musical instruments. I cannot help it if all the rest is 'charm.' A lot of what I did later was charm. Everything Braque did later was charm too... Of course one can sleep with a prostitute and get a lot of pleasure out of it, but one must realize she is a prostitute. Vice and virtue are two different things... You must tell the truth about the Louvre because you know it. Prostitutes, pretty prostitutes, but nothing more. Cubism alone produced painting."

One may consider these statements as mere witticisms. But let us imagine for a moment that the art displayed in museums is no longer the object of a cult and that one views the act of painting as Picasso does, isolating its ideological and sentimental content, which from the aesthetic viewpoint is not only legitimate but necessary. Classical painting now appears to one as a collection of refined techniques: modelling, shading and aerial perspective, chiaroscuro, scumbling and glazing. And, no matter how different are the works in which they are employed, they *all* tend towards a certain type of *trompe-l'œil*, imitating the natural continuities and the impressions of optical blending produced by the human eye. From Leonardo to Corot, from Rubens to Monet, traditional painters created, in the face of obvious conventions, materialized reflexes that simulate a presence. Behind the surface of the picture (and perhaps that is what reveals its quality) we can sense something beyond the image: the soul of Mona Lisa, the misty light of Mortefontaine, a memory of waterlilies at sunset.

But of a sudden Picasso and the Cubists set themselves to analyse space and split it up into its various elements. As a result, the discontinuity that had till then been invisible, or rather *concealed by technical artifices*, penetrated to the heart of the plastic structure. Broken contours, dislocated planes, substances and colors divorced from form, light that radiates not from a natural or artificial source but from the canvas itself, all these things baffled a spectator uprooted from the cosy world to which he was accustomed. There was no mistaking this: Cubism opposed a deliberate non-resemblance to the refinements, which in ultimate analysis are naïve, of illusionism. A jumble of super-posed planes, a bit of simulated wood, a rectangle or dirty rag, anything you like, can represent a guitar—anything but the exact image of that guitar.

Debat-Ponsan, a "master of the Belle Epoque" who specialized in painting cows at pasture, never let an unfinished picture leave his studio. This was the amazing reason he gave: "In that state anybody could steal my methods." How then can it surprise us that at the outset Cubism was synonymous with the systematic destruction of the trickery of the image? But must that lead to the conclusion that since then nothing has counted but "signs"? Picasso assures us that "a painting is a legible sign like those that mark one-way streets." But when we compare Cubist signs with those of the highway code or even with those of the ancient code of heraldry, we are struck by the obvious indigence of utilitarian signs. Cubist signs too are poor compared with the images of traditional painting, but they are amazingly rich in comparison with non-aesthetic signs. The pressure brought to bear at present by the fashion for linguistics in favor of the assimilation of art to a "language" can do nothing to diminish this discrepancy.

"This painting is to the other as poetry is to prose," wrote Juan Gris of Cubism. That formula should be pondered. It should be shaded too, perhaps, for every art is unjust towards its predecessor. Can one honestly maintain that Leonardo, Rembrandt, Renoir, even Ingres himself, were merely prose writers of the image? What, on the other hand, can hardly be denied, except on rare occasions, is that their art—like that of Racine or Victor Hugo—relies on the tricks of rhetoric. What it owes to plastic arrangement can never be clearly distinguished from the allurements of the subject and the fascination of the handling. It is poetry, of course, but it depends to a great extent on obvious borrowings from and evident allusions to its cultural environment. A Cubist work, instead, aims at having no reference points outside itself. "The subject," said Braque, "is like a fog that has lifted allowing the objects to appear."

It is only the unitary conception of a culture dominated by the written word—and Pierre Francastel denounced this long ago—that could forge so close a link between poetry and language while denying it the crystallization of meaning and the reversion to primordial ambiguity which precede all fixed order. Strictly speaking, one might perhaps be justified in assimilating Cubism to a sort of code as far as some of the minor followers of that movement are concerned, but ceaseless renovation of the "signs" is the most unquestionable aspect of Picasso's art. This is so true that people have been led to term versatility what in that artist is permanent creation.

This, no doubt, is one more reason not to evade the problem raised by Picasso's Ingrism. In fact, that inveterate iconoclast, that inventor of an art which is at the antipodes of "image-making," has never ceased to display, all through his oeuvre, what appears to be a nostalgia for the image. From 1917 right up to his most recent drawings we can see him dabble—alongside his cruel inventions—with the old, classical idioms, parody their humanist accents in a half-ironical, half-serious manner, connive deliberately with what he calls "charm."

Indeed, has he not reproached himself for his infidelity to the spirit of Cubism? In 1948, commenting on one of the *collages* he did in 1914, he confessed to the sculptor Henri Laurens: "We must have been crazy—or cowardly—to give up all that! We had wonderful resources... and I reverted to oil and you to marble. It's crazy!"

Never has the interplay of the two aesthetics between which Picasso's work is unequally divided been so subtle or produced such happy results as in the last twenty years. During that time he has increasingly mingled with the coherent processes of plastic art his own fanciful themes and mythology, which still baffle us by setting their living paradoxes against so many conscientious anticonformisms. "We must kill off modern art," he is fond of saying, "for once again it is no longer modern."

Should we conclude, as do certain critics who breathlessly pursue the latest vogue, that "the Picasso exhibition (of 1966-1967) showed him to be half a century behind living art"? What if that art is less "living" than some people think? What if the padded tedium of the art galleries contains more of the Bouguereaus and Domergues of tomorrow than they imagine? Today great painters come thirteen to the dozen, a fact that in itself should give us food for thought. One can readily understand that some people are in a hurry to place Picasso's art in the great museum of History and smother it in flowers, but obviously it cannot be accommodated in one of the standard rooms where they seemingly want to confine Cubism ("born 1907, died 1914").

"In my eyes," said Picasso no later than 1923, "art has neither past nor future. If a work of art is unable to live always in the present it is not worth considering. The art of the Greeks, the Egyptians, the great painters who lived in other days, is not an art of the past: it is perhaps more alive today than ever before... All I have ever done I have done for the present, in the hope that it will always remain in the present."

"In the present." Too little attention has been paid to this singular aspect of Cubism. For Cubism not only reinvented the arts that, like the arts of primitive peoples, lie outside history; it also, when it "invented" the Douanier Rousseau, discovered the art that lies outside culture, namely naïve art. These arts, as Claude Lévi-Strauss has said, are the only ones that "do not grow old" because they are timeless and unconnected with any social reality. To a certain extent this is true of Cubism too. Consequently, what you will find here is less a history than a description. If a Cubist work is a sign—or even a pseudo-sign— the first thing for us to do is to describe its significant elements. Rather than offer, after so many others, a new, uncertain image of Picasso, I propose to take a good look at some of his works.

PORTRAITS OF WOMEN

Portraiture long since lost its traditional function of preserving an image, but its celebrative character is still intact and, indeed, enhanced. "I put into my painting everything I love," says Picasso, for whom objectivity is what matters least. Under these conditions, what happens to resemblance, to "lifelikeness"? One would be wrong to say that it disappears, but it ceases to be naïve.

These three portraits of Hélène Parmelin, Sylvette and Jacqueline differ considerably though they were painted within a brief space of time. Picasso endeavored by obvious variations in handling to fix their profound individuality, but in this case the term "profundity" has a different meaning. His aim was not to interpret the "soul" of his sitter: Mona Lisa no longer smiles. The "psychology" of which Classicism was so fond has yielded to an assemblage of plastic accents that situate the individual in space: they give her a permanent expression no less inalienable than her bearing or her smile, and no less worthy of our notice than her changing state of mind.

"Yes, I did it in a quarter of an hour," said Matisse of one of his drawings, "but with the experience of a whole lifetime." It matters little whether the model is present in the flesh or merely in the artist's memory. The original sensation that emanates from him can only be communicated by the forms of a *handwriting*.

Thus the portrait of *Madame H.P.* (Hélène Parmelin, wife of Picasso's friend the painter Edouard Pignon) is essentially linear.

PORTRAIT OF MADAME H.P., 1952. OIL AND ENAMEL PAINT ON PLYWOOD

PORTRAIT OF MADEMOISELLE D. (SYLVETTE) IN SIDE VIEW, APRIL 29, 1954. OIL.

As often occurs where Picasso is concerned, the task of the color is to heighten the drawing by stressing the contrast between flesh, dress and hair. It does not produce an illusion nor suggest an imaginary space; it performs the primary function of what Léger called "enlivening surfaces."

Shortly after his break with Françoise Gilot, Picasso painted a series of eighteen portraits of Sylvette, a fair-haired young girl of the type one saw around Saint-Germain-des-Prés twenty years ago. At Vallauris everyone called her "the English girl" and as a model she was dangerously pretty. Since art has no worse enemy than prettiness, Picasso did not shrink, in some pictures of the series, from covering the entire face with one sweeping stroke of the brush.

The portrait of Sylvette (Mademoiselle D.) reproduced here is one of those that make the greatest concessions to "charm." It displays a few reminiscences of Cubist forms in the rendering of the dress and still more in the combination of front face and profile, which in this case results rather in a double profile. This typical convention of Cubism has been variously interpreted. Does it, as we have been told, aim at conveying the maximum of information on the object by noting successive points of view? Or is it not rather a question of granting the form a certain freedom in space and avoiding the effect of a flattened image produced by a single viewpoint, common alike to classical painting and the camera eye?

The most recent of the three portraits is that of *Jacqueline with Clasped Hands*, which served as poster for the "Homage to Picasso" exhibition. It is undoubtedly the most highly worked up as well as the most remarkable for the concurrence of the model's expression with the handwriting utilized to render it. Unlike the other two, this work develops in a three-dimensional space and displays the forms of Picasso's latest Cubist phase reduced to the utmost simplification.

PORTRAIT OF JACQUELINE WITH CLASPED HANDS, JUNE 3, 1954. OIL.

The technique employed in the portrait of Hélène Parmelin (oil and enamel paint on plywood) suggests with its large patches of flat color volumes without depth. The posture of the figure firmly anchored to the ground, with the legs at right angles and the left arm providing an additional prop, produces a massive presence that is a frequent feature of Picasso's work. The sitter's individuality is further stressed by the huge crop of copper-colored hair, its anarchic disorder rendered by hard, angular lines; it fills the whole picture with its dazzling brightness.

In the elegant portrait of Sylvette, the excessive purity of the Greek profile avoids "prettiness" thanks to the Cubist doubling of the traditional image, and so remains acceptable in the transition from nature to art. The conventionally velvety modelling expresses, as in the portraits of his daughter Maia as a child (1938), the freshness of extreme youth. The two diverging perspectives of the rocking-chair suggest an enveloping movement around the all too graceful silhouette.

In the portrait of Jacqueline, the elongation of the neck, still more marked than in the preceding work, is all the more noticeable in that the body is huddled on the ground with the knees drawn up to the chest and the hands and feet barely indicated. The neck and hair proclaim the sovereign indifference of all statuesque beauty, evoking the precise geometry of a "welded sheet-metal cut-out" that gives the face, with its huge eye, a monumental relief.

This "painted sculpture" is still painting in so far as the surrounding space is not sacrificed. Divided into alternately dark and light sectors that radiate from the head, that space hints at a classically pyramidal composition, which is balanced on the left by two squares placed one above the other and emphasized by contrasts of color. A few blacks and the thick reds of the Provençal floor tiles set off the fresh colors of the sitter's dress. The handwriting is austere but shows no trace of cruelty.

Picasso is not what one calls a *portrait painter*. In these three works he has renounced the kaleidoscope of naïve resemblance and given the encounter with the individual a universal significance. But the conventions he invents are far less gratuitous than some people think. He can say without a hint of irony: "When I have something to say, I say it in the way I find most natural."

GOAT SKULL, MAY 14, 1952. AQUATINT.

STILL LIFE

NEVER have still lifes less deserved that name. Not that Picasso attempts, like Chardin, to depict the soul of things. In his eyes to "paint the invisible" would be utopistic: he is really and truly interested only in forms. It is through still lifes that the Cubists first became aware that they wanted to eliminate the distance that separates the spectator from the spectacle and "touch the object." "When a still life is no longer within arm's reach," Braque told Dora Vallier, "it ceases to be a still life." One tends to imagine the painter taking the object as his starting point and transposing it in a subjective vision. What really happens is just the opposite: in Braque's words, "the object can only appear in so far as the painting allows it to... There is no question of starting out from the object: one goes towards the object. What interests us is the path one takes to go towards the object." A comparison between three still lifes of 1951-1952 in which the subject is the same will enable us to realize how different that path can be.

If comparing the aquatint entitled *Goat Skull* with the painting that follows it, we call the first "naturalistic" or "realistic," what do we mean exactly by those terms? Let us imagine the print while it was being executed: obviously the drawing is modelled on the object, aims at suggesting its real substance and form and, to a certain extent, its *presence*. There is no use reopening the pointless debate on realism. But, however much one insists on the part played by interpretation and the intervention of the artist's hand, there is undoubtedly a certain familiar relationship between the work and reality. A material, but superfluous demonstration of this could be obtained by superposing on the aquatint a photograph taken from the same angle. *Saving its technical limitations*, a work of this type establishes an optical reflex with regard to which the artist has left himself very little scope for intervention. No doubt appreciation of the work involves precisely perceiving that margin, but such perception by no means excludes the reflex effect and the sensation of a presence. Baudelaire quite rightly saw in western realism a suggestive magic that exploits the forces of the image.

It is not enough to say that the painting entitled *Goat Skull, Bottle and Candle* is "more freely interpreted" than the print we have just discussed. Here, in fact, there is no longer any question of an image that deceives the eye; it is not the object that *seems* to be present but the "painting" that thrusts its own presence on our attention, tangibly, at the object's expense. The divergencies from reality do not depend on limitations but on choices: they are no longer technical but aesthetic. What counts most is not their objective value but their *intentional* character.

Whereas the aquatint aimed at a resemblance, however personally interpreted, the painting aspires first and foremost to a non-resemblance. Nothing in nature suggested to Picasso the convention of the triple contour (two black outlines limiting one white), the division of space into curvilinear triangles and trapezoids, the arbitrary distribution of highlights and shadows. Analytic Cubism fragmented the planes in a space that was undoubtedly conventional, but no less aerial for that. Here space is flat: it is the space of a shattered mirror. The traits that could still be observed, so to say, objectively in the print—the marked convexity of the nosebone, the eye socket that forms a white ledge, the flattened front teeth, the dislocation of the jaw bone—appear in the painting as clear, or at least recognizable, elements of the design, like the various elements of a sign. The loss of resemblance is made up for by the enhanced *plastic intensity* in accordance with the paradox, which we can do no more than state, that "in art the simpler the means, the more evident the sensibility" (Gustave Moreau).

GOAT SKULL, BOTTLE AND CANDLE, 1952. OIL.

GOAT SKULL AND BOTTLE, 1951-1952. PAINTED BRONZE.

The third of these works, *Goat Skull and Bottle*, is a sculptured still life in which Picasso has utilized plastic metaphors like that of the famous *Bull's Head with a Bicycle Seat*. The flame of the candle is represented by a circular object pierced with long needles that stand for the light rays. The animal's skull is modelled with pieces of corrugated cardboard whose torn and uneven surface is reminiscent of the procedures designated in architecture by the term brutalism. The eyes are the heads of big bolts and the horns are once again a pair of bicycle handlebars. The plastic sign springs directly from the objects, which seem all the more opaque in that they are placed in an unexpected context, deprived of their natural function and uprooted from the world of utility.

These three still lifes offer us three different paths to "go towards the object." The first is the traditional one, whose essential naivety is corrected by the ingenuity of the techniques employed. It is the path of imitation and rather than "going towards the object" starts out from it.

The second elaborates a plastic construction which is hard to define because it lies *midway between sign and image*; it is just as far from the literal prose of the utilitarian sign as from the diffuse poetry of the traditional image. In a work of this type poetry breaks free from the "fog of the subject" to pervade an aggregate of raw plastic elements

This raw aspect, which can already be observed in the *papiers collés* and the "object constructions" Picasso produced between 1911 and 1913, is most clearly perceptible in the third still life. Here the plastic sign lies midway between the traditional sculptured image and the utilitarian object that apparently lacks all aesthetic value. The importance of these assemblages of unorthodox materials is comparable with that of the *papiers collés* and their occurrence was an outstanding event in the history of sculpture.

In a world in which objects loom larger and larger, Picasso's art endeavors to extract from an association with the strange yet familiar universe of things a new sort of poetry, that is to say, of happiness. The effort of the artist who wrests objects from their utilitarian environment parallels that of the poet who frees words from their customary use. This reversion to the raw and the elementary counters alienation by the commonplace object. The very appearance of the deliberately rough, haphazard products of this art tends to deny the smooth functional world, whose perfectly adapted "social language" besets us in our daily life. The artist employs bits and pieces of trash to suggest *the object's return to nature*. Opaque and meaningless, having no justification but that conferred upon it by the artist, the object eludes the demands of the social "language" and attains what André Breton called the "wild state."

So it is a mistake to consider such constructions as "monstrous." As Kahnweiler said, "Once the picture is composed, it may happen that the spectator naïvely confuses sign and sense. That is just what a person does who considers monstrous one of Picasso's figures, and I really mean that the person who says he loves the monstrosity he 'sees' (even if he speaks of 'convulsive beauty') is no less naïve than the one who turns away from it in disgust. In both persons this confusion is the result of the habit of establishing the identity of a plastic sign with its sense." In other words, the Cubist aesthetic repudiates the *pseudo-presence of the sense* in order to stress the *presence of the sign*. "They have called us abstract," said Braque. But all art is in fact concrete. Cubism asserts, with a sort of discriminating brutalism, the substance and the plastic essence of the sign: it is a *realism of the significant element*.

There is no exaggerating the importance of this revolution. Poetry ousted rhetoric. The image aimed at persuading or seducing. The ambiguity of the sign casts a spell.

"LOFTY SENTIMENTS"

Picasso has been criticized, in the name of a purism that is at least arguable, for his "reversions to the subject." But how can one possibly mix up "program art" with the rare moments when it suddenly becomes obvious that art must give way to higher values and sacrifice a fraction of the purity of its message to the demands of communication? In fact, there is no danger of seeing Picasso permanently wave a flag. We must applaud the rarity of his professions of faith no less than the energy with which he pronounces them. *Guernica, The Charnel House, Massacre in Korea, The Fall of Icarus, The Temple of Peace,* may not seem much. But they are a great deal when we think of the many other works in which commitment is totally ignored.

"The 'lofty sentiments'," wrote Kahnweiler, "which Picasso has mentioned to me so often as one of his ambitions in art, culminate in pity or, more precisely, in a less mawkish sentiment, namely 'respect'—respect for other people." And he added: "Today millions of people know Picasso as the creator of the Dove of Peace, as the man of peace; and in so doing they are infinitely nearer to the real Picasso than those stunted aesthetes who delight only in certain of his pictures, seeing nothing but colored surfaces without objective significance, and who turn away in disgust from *Massacre in Korea*."

Yet the color scheme of the latter is no less deliberately austere than that of *Guernica*: the butchers and their victims stand out in the same drab tone against the monotone green of the ravaged countryside and the dirty grey of the sky. On one hand, the breastplates, helmets and iron masks that represent blind, all-destroying violence; on the other, the bare face of innocence. Is this rhetoric? Or merely the eloquence of a universal language? In the UNESCO building in Paris, half hidden by a stepped gangway, the work for which Georges Salles suggested the title *The Fall of Icarus* spreads its vast area. As usual, Picasso has given no hint as to the significance of the black form foundering in the blue sea; it might equally well symbolize War, Death or the forces of Evil. The scenery for the ballet *Icare* staged by Serge Lifar in the Paris Opera House in 1962 was far more explicit and proved that Picasso's interest in the theater has never flagged.

Most important of all is the *Temple of Peace* at Vallauris, of which Picasso said in 1952: "I must do it now while I am still able to climb a ladder." It was a bold venture to decorate a place with so little atmosphere, a casemate or ossuary whose vaulted ceiling rises only some ten feet above the floor. The work is brought to life by the sole magic of the execution; the visitor is assaulted by the monumental figures inserted in a rigorous composition. Here we find no backward glance towards Byzantium, Pompeii or Christian art: we are immersed in an exclusively Picassian, twentieth-century universe.

The picture on the left-hand side shows us the pageant of *War*. The War God, enthroned on the box seat of a hearse drawn by black horses whose hooves trample on the Book of Knowledge which is half consumed by fire, is backed by sinister shades. In the very center of the composition the sword of vanquished war is poised above the blood-soaked earth. On the left stands the young Soldier of Peace, holding in one hand the scales of Justice, in the other a pure white shield blazoned with a Dove; his gigantic stature dominates the forces of Evil and protects the crops of Peace.

THE TEMPLE OF PEACE, VALLAURIS, 1952. OVERALL VIEW.

On the opposite wall, under a huge multicolored sun, whose rays are leafy branches, are displayed the toils and sports of *Peace*. A man is busying himself beside a rustic hearth; close by a group of women are reading, drawing or giving suck. In the center, a great white Pegasus draws a plough guided by a child.

THE TEMPLE OF PEACE, VALLAURIS: THE SOLDIER OF PEACE, 1952.
DETAIL OF THE LEFT SIDE.

On the left are two dancing women, one of whom balances on her forefinger the aerial structure of a living "mobile" which consists of a child with an owl perched on his head, an hourglass, a bird-cage and a goldfish bowl. As in a poem by Prévert, the birds are in the bowl and the fish in the cage: the age-old dream of a "topsy-turvy world" expresses freedom from care.

Here the bold inventions that were a feature of Cubism have been harnessed to the flowing style of a large-scale mural decoration whose first aim is to be intelligible to all. As in *Guernica*, contours and colors, highlights and shadows, derive from sign painting, though here the signs have no surprises in store for us. But whereas in *The Charnel House* and *Massacre in Korea* we find the same grey monochrome as in that masterpiece of 1937, the *Temple of Peace* reflects an optimistic frame of mind and explodes in brightly colored blotches (the sun, an orange tree) over a group of ochre and greyish-white figures.

Of course there is no avoiding a comparison with the vast spaces placed at Matisse's disposal in his chapel at Vence. There the broad panels of white ceramic tiles reflect the iridescent tints of the stained-glass windows; whereas Picasso took up the challenge of a space that is totally enclosed. Vence and Vallauris: two temperaments so far apart that one excludes the other. On the one hand the peaceful, airy space of a refuge, a twentieth-century Port-Royal. On the other a space overwhelmed by the weight of the vaulted ceiling, and its dramatic division into two parts, the pleasures of Peace and the terrors of War, seems to reflect the dualism of Picasso's entire oeuvre. "There's no serenity for me," was his reply when Gide said to him: "We have reached the age of serenity." His art bears witness to a latent *Angst*, which it tries to evade by dazzling ploys that it would be wrong to call meaningless. Love of life is only achieved by overcoming the agony of life. Under the vaulted ceiling of Vallauris the sole images of happiness are work and play.

GOAT, 1950. BRONZE.

What is a goat for Picasso? Suspended from its vertebral axis (which is made out of the central rib of a palm leaf), a sort of wine-skin with a quantity of excrescences balances the massive, bony, obstinate head. The detail of the material is no less suggestive: here a rectilinear fragment marks the slanting ridge of the neck; there the interlacings of a scrap of basketwork are the tactile equivalent of a skinny flank; there again a couple of pieces of pottery mimic the heavy, swollen udders.

SCULPTURE

ABOUT 1950 Picasso suddenly created a whole sculptured menagerie that makes a curious impact on the spectator. Till then animals had occupied a very secondary place in his work. Of course the set of aquatints for Buffon's *Histoire Naturelle* published by Vollard in 1937 shows that they interested him up to a point; but as a rule he seldom ventured beyond the familiar sphere of the bullfight except when he rediscovered in his famous Doves of Peace the memory of the pigeons his father used to paint when he was a child. It may have been that his irrepressible vitality was content just then to restrict its outbursts to the shadowy zone between man and beast, giving birth to the convulsive monsters of the Fables or inventing "metamorphoses" that even the most daring surgeons had never dreamt of. Unless, perhaps, he preferred to find expression, as at Antibes, in the euphemism of a stylized mythology. Be that as it may, after 1950 a whole menagerie issued forth from the Ark: *The Goat, The Monkey and Her Baby, The Crane*, and whole flocks of *Doves* and *Owls*.

"Greece," said Jean Giraudoux, "is a lot of kings and goats scattered around on marble." In classical art the goat symbolized Arcadia and conjured up a pastoral way of life. In Picasso's case, if the draughtsman often takes pleasure in allusive details, the sculptor prefers, as if he too had just left the Ark, to explore with his fingers an elementary, primordial world of long-forgotten forms.

A huge earthen jar or pot forms the body of this *Monkey*. Two metal handles do duty for ears. The tail is an old metal spring. The head is worth examining in detail: we recognize two little toy motorcars, one above the other, which give the animal an intense, yet indefinable expression. We can read it equally well as a mother's tenderness or as ferocity towards a possible attacker. This is a twentieth-century version of the "Mother and Child" theme renovated by a use of ready-made objects that has nothing in common with those of Marcel Duchamp.

THE MONKEY AND HER BABY, 1952. BRONZE.

THE MONKEY AND HER BABY (DETAIL), 1952. BRONZE.

A common gas cock in which Picasso inserted a bit of pointed metal does duty very well for the feathery crest and mobile head of a *Crane*. The blade of a shovel forms the tail, while the bird's cautious, mincing gait is expressed by a couple of forks resting on their prongs. The plumage of the *Angry Owl* is made of bent or broken old nails fixed seemingly at haphazard on the modelled mass of the body. This work, while expressing very cogently the disorder of the bird's bristling feathers, has also the unusual aspect of a figurine used in black magic. What could be less naturalistic than that?

◄ THE CRANE, 1952. PAINTED BRONZE.

ANGRY OWL, 1953. BRONZE.

A very commonplace scene—Françoise Gilot pushing little Claude's pram—gave Picasso the cue for a hieratic Mother and Child, a sort of primitive idol with the head of a giant ant. On a rigid bust formed by one of those ornamental cast-iron plaques that used to embellish open hearths and kitchen stoves, two cake tins represent the breasts in hollow relief. The whole structure rests on a metal tube, upright like a pillar, which stands for the skirt. These objects, which were made for other purposes, enabled Picasso to renew the immemorial dialogue between the sculptor and the human form.

WOMAN WITH A PRAM
(DETAIL), 1950. BRONZE.

WOMAN WITH A PRAM, 1950. BRONZE.

Like any other piece of non-monumental sculpture, we must view *The Goat* from close up if we are to discern what it is made of. When we do so, we discover that it is anything but a feat of skill by a naturalistic animal sculptor.

In 1945, when he executed *Man with a Sheep*, Picasso still employed the traditional method of modelling, which consisted in covering up a framework. Now it is the framework itself that becomes sculpture—an assemblage of bits of wood, basketwork and pottery held together with a little plastic paste. Picasso eliminates the "skin of things" to reveal their essential architecture. The result is a quantity of forms, at once familiar and ignored, which he rescues from the insipidity of the commonplace and restores to the truth of sensation.

Whether these apparently crude techniques involve fragments or entire identifiable objects, Picasso knows how to make them express the subtlest shades of meaning. Cocteau called this "a rag-picker's art," but its quality makes it worthy of consideration. The quest for unexpected affinities among things found in the flea-market seemingly confirms what Lévi-Strauss said when he likened the artist's procedure to tinkering. But compared with the whimsical creations of the tinker, which are imbued with the bumbling yet touching poetry of failure, the artist's success gives the impression of an absolute value. The tinker makes a clumsy attempt to transform ill-adapted "functions"; the artist, beyond the function, re-creates form.

In spite of Picasso's protests, critics have insisted on likening these plastic metaphors to the *collages* of the Surrealists. This involved ignoring the fact that a *collage* (which Aragon rightly distinguishes from a *papier collé*) is essentially an "intellectual game" that takes advantage of an unusual contrast of meanings to create artificially an "objective hazard" (like the "encounter of an umbrella and a sewing machine on a dissecting table"). "Object sculpture" is quite the contrary: it is a "plastic game" which ironically ignores semantic dissonances and makes use of the unforeseeable correspondences of forms. It inserts intellectual negation in plastic affirmation.

This art, which is intensely expressive but avoids the unconvincing outbursts of Expressionism, opposes the objectivity of forms that are stable *because* pre-existent to lyrical distortions. How can we possibly contest these forms, which Picasso, the archaeologist of the commonplace, extracts from the magma of meanings? There they have always been before our eyes but we have failed to see them. Once removed from their normal context, they receive the strange gift of remaining refractory to the world of "style," resistant to the rapid wear that threatens all figuration, indefinitely expressive because indefinitely disconcerting. The little motorcar never quite becomes a monkey's head, just as the bicycle saddle never quite became the bull's head. By losing its identity and eluding classification the object reverts to the wild state. Whenever Picasso tackles a new work he sweeps away all he knows and focuses his attention on what he feels, and touches. Like a blind Minotaur in a new world, he explores forms he has never met with before.

PLAYING BATHER, 1958. BRONZE.

GEOMETRY IN SPACE

THE object sculptures evaded the control of the line by a rather singular use of the manufactured object. Instead, some more recent works have opted for a manifest geometry. This is true of *Bathers*, a group of six figures composed solely of straight lines and Euclidean forms, as well as of an amusing *Playing Bather*.

A *Head* of 1958 is a striking example of this formula. The three-dimensional tin guitars and the "object constructions" of 1912 displayed a complex interplay of planes of different colors; here instead we are confronted by crude forms and an insistence on the material that makes this *Head* a sculpture in the fullest sense of the word. The sign is made manifest through the resistance of a coarse material, which will strike the spectator (whose broad smile or exaggerated gravity are equally symptomatic of the inertia of a certain culture) either by its contrast with the subject or by its connivance with the pitiless reduction of the forms to their most elementary expression.

In fact, even the simplest work does more than propound a style: it inevitably involves an aesthetic. This *Head* owes its value to the obvious difficulty of placing it in any of the accepted categories. Is it Surrealist, Dadaist, Cubist? Where is the dream fantasy or the premeditated intellectual insolence—the eyes of Mona Lisa, the wig of "real hair"—that would justify the Surrealist label? It is closer perhaps to the destructive humor of Dada, in so far as the choice of worthless materials (a piece of discarded timber, buttons in the place of eyes) and the deliberate crudeness of the construction suggest the intention to make a mockery of art. But, though there is no denying the general influence of both Dadaism and Surrealism, one is no less warranted—for borderline works demonstrate both the necessity and the relativity of classification—in viewing it as a critical phase of Cubist austerity: the three-sided conjunction of a *concept*, a *form* and a *material* treated in a manner calculated to produce not traditional harmony but a visible tension. The concept is reduced to the commonest anthropological notion, the form to a schematic geometry, the material to the most commonplace things. Far removed from the subtle compromises of traditional Painting and Sculpture, this terroristic work confronts the humanistic allurements of Culture with a sort of elementary human sign, akin to the archaic creations of which Baudelaire said that "an inevitable, synthetic, infantile barbarism often remains visible in a perfect art."

Nowhere can we see so clearly the resistance to sense characteristic of the Cubist signs in which the material uses its roughness to oppose the encroachment of the concept. The rich messages of classical art offered "redundant" images that were wide open to culture's fluid meanings, which submerged them in a prating rhetoric. Both Canova's stammering idylls and Rodin's roaring epics offered messages without any signs other than the literary signs of their setting. Here, instead, a voiceless sculpture

Doesn't this *Head* remind you of a bootblack's box? A work of this sort derives its singular expression from the borderline position it occupies between the total opacity of the object (a small packing case) and the conceptual transparency of the sign. No four-year-old wandering through an exhibition could fail to recognize it at first glance as a "man" and identify its sign with those he draws himself.

HEAD, CANNES, 1958. BRONZE.

BATHERS, 1956. BRONZE.

These *Bathers* elude cold abstraction by a sort of uncouth fixity or barbaric hieraticism which contrasts with their humorous attitudes; this is clear to see in *Man with Clasped Hands*, in the *Diver* and still more in the *Man-Fountain*. Besides, the aggressively crude nature of the materials employed —packing-case slats, painter's canvas stretcher, the feet of a couch (in the *Diver* on the far left)—would suffice to exorcise the rigor of this spatial geometry. In the *Playing Bather* (page 50) it is the exact symmetry of the volumes that gives the geometry its comic aspect.

that retreats into itself rediscovers the admirable quality of silence we find in the art of primitive peoples. Messages without signs are replaced by signs without a message.

There is a profound analogy between Cubist creation and poetic creation. When Picasso, with an awkwardness he makes no attempt to conceal, cuts out pieces of wood to form a head or discovers a form in the seams of a plaster cast, in the hazards of a laceration or a cut-out, he acts like a poet who prefers the chancy structure of signs to the false certainty of meanings. "One must," said Mallarmé, "restore the initiative to the word."

WOMAN AND DWARF CLOWN, 1953. WASH DRAWING.

IRONIC CONFIDINGS

THERE is such a thing as "naïve painting" but no such thing as "naïve drawing." Drawing is mobile, subtle, closely akin to writing, capable of the most breath-taking ellipses. It suggests more than it expresses and lends itself to hints and suggestions. Picasso, who is neither a purist nor an aesthete, has done a great deal of book illustration. This shows how willing he is on occasion to subordinate plastic expression to literature. And where he feels able to do without the pretext of a written text, he draws his private diary ("Executing a work is a way of keeping one's diary." — Picasso to Tériade in 1932).

In the space of two months (from November 23, 1953, to February 3, 1954) Picasso did no less than a hundred and eighty pen drawings on the theme of the Old Painter and his Model. They reveal a new accentuation. Irony conceals the secrets confided and exploits a contrast: the contrast between the aged painter of the academic type, long-haired, short-sighted, meticulous, engrossed in his palette and his canvas—some of the drawings show us grotesque art-lovers examining the latter with a magnifying glass—and the young model who nonchalantly displays her splendid, sensuous beauty.

On occasion the ironic distance is stressed by certain elements of the theme and the works in which this occurs are undoubtedly the strangest and the most engaging. The Old Painter is replaced by the Old Clown: satire, quite literally, dons a mask. In fact, the mask of the Harlequins of the rose period reappears in this

IN THE STUDIO, JANUARY 10, 1954, XIV. WASH DRAWING.

In some drawings, to confirm the satirical value of the theme, the old painter is replaced by a monkey perched on a stool. What we have here is the satirical, almost bitter replica, after an interval of twenty years, of the etchings Picasso did in 1933 on the theme of the Sculptor's Workshop in which the sculptor, bearded like an ancient Greek, and his surfeited model were lost in a voluptuous, vaguely contemplative repose. There the artist used an antiquarian fiction to mark his detachment from real or simulated autobiography. Here he is quite satisfied with irony alone.

long series as a prop in a decor that presents us with variants that have an almost structural exactness. Here the Old Man and the Young Woman wear the masks of the characters they represent; there, unable to swop ages, they swop masks. Here the Saltimbanque removes his mask revealing a face made up like

THE MONKEY AND THE MASK, JANUARY 25, 1954, II. WASH DRAWING.

TWO FIGURES, JANUARY 27, 1954, XIV. COLOR CRAYONS.

that of an actor in the Japanese No plays; there the old dwarf
clown, his face hidden by a mask, is depicted gazing in ecstasy
at a beauty who is close yet cruelly out of reach. Some sheets
show us the Young Woman playing nonchalantly with fluttering
Cupids, a cat or a pet monkey, displaying an animal innocence

that makes the aging man feel like an outsider. Elsewhere the Old Man and the Young Girl talk together like children on their best behavior. In one colored crayon drawing entitled *Two Figures*, the same fresh green and acrid pink are used to render the Old Man's grin and the Young Girl's inimitable posture — arms hugging knees, head held effortlessly erect — which calls to mind a tamed animal, or perhaps one ready to take flight. Is this a farewell to love? Or a new-fangled pastime suggested by an Art of Love for the Aged?

The dazzling cleverness of the drawing defies analysis. Overcoming the apparent banality of the subject, the linework captures with a staggering accuracy here a pouting lip, there a jaunty hat, there again the insolent or unconscious elegance of a pose or a torso—everywhere the almost ferociously humorous contrast between age and youth, ugliness and beauty. This series has a place of its own in Picasso's oeuvre. Taking advantage of the ease with which drawing can trace ill-defined frontiers, it marks no doubt the utmost limit of the concessions art can make to anecdote. Here we are midway between the permissiveness of the picturesque and the exigencies of pure line drawing. The quality of the penmanship employed in the service of a razor-sharp humor prevents this series from resembling the glib drawings affected by cartoonists. Nonetheless, the ellipse—for the technique of point-and-line drawing naturally calls for an elliptic treatment—never aims at an arbitrarily static sign but always at a dynamically expressive gesture. No matter how condensed the richness typical of realistic notation may be, the direct allusion to real life and the effect of immediate presence never give way entirely to the handwriting. This type of drawing, like a shorthand script jotted down from life, remains bound up with the image.

In contrast to the satirical series we have just discussed, the extremely pure line of a lithograph entitled *The Bull Game*

THE BULL GAME, FEBRUARY 14, 1954. LITHOGRAPH.

(February 14, 1954) is a perfect illustration of what it has been agreed to term Picasso's "Ingrism" (or "Neo-Classicism"). It is a convenient label, but as a matter of fact Picasso's drawing differs substantially from that of Ingres, not so much in certain distortions that are more Cubist than Ingresque—the left shoulder of the man with the bull's head mask, the full-face/ profile of the nymph in the foreground—as in the less dry and more mobile line as well as in a greater disregard for lifelikeness. Thus in the group of the three women, a choreographic figure that simulates flight, the enlaced bodies contract or dilate to suit

BULLFIGHT SCENE, FEBRUARY 25, 1960, VIII. WASH DRAWING.

BACCHANAL, 1955. INDIAN INK AND GOUACHE.

On the horizon a small section of the murky sky brightens to set off
the faces and gestures of the two principal actors. The gouache throws
a wan light of a different quality on the figure of the Bacchante whose
expressive, twisted posture displays her armpits and her dishevelled hair.
The figures fill the picture plane in a manifest *horror vacui* which reveals
a certain indifference towards the expression of space. But through the
cultural conventions of this studied work we are made aware of a temperament: the Mediterranean myth recovers the vigor of a primitive cult.

the requirements of the action (cf. the two characters in the middle distance). It is a "game" of conventional gestures and faultless linework—there is not a single correction in the hair, hands or faces—but lacks the sharp tension of Ingresque realism. In particular, it makes no concessions to what the naïve art-lover calls life. This spare handwriting on the pure white sheet of paper constitutes a reversion to the austerity, the asceticism of great art after the interlude of satirical recreation; conforming with the aesthetic peculiar to line drawing, it conjures up forms without substance. Nothing could be more fitting than this deliberate emptiness for a ballet danced on a timeless stage by a weightless humanity.

Does the draughtsman's art achieve density by exchanging patches for lines? Be that as it may, Picasso explored the expressive possibilities of "tachist" drawing in a series of wash and Indian ink drawings done in 1959-1960, which Michel Leiris entitled *Le Romancero du Picador*. One must peruse these sheets as one would a storybook. Most of them represent that pariah of the bull-ring, the picador, "the man who hits below the belt," at the moment of the *suerte de picas*. The technique of deliberate patches and blots leaves something no less deliberately to chance. Accidents turn into accents and the random becomes expressive thanks to the rapid movement of the brush.

Picasso is sufficiently interested in drawing and engraving to make frequent use of composite techniques. A work in Indian ink heightened with gouache, entitled *Bacchanal*, combines the procedures of wash drawing, pen-and-ink and gouache in a splendid composition, in which there is not a single empty space, forcefully centered on Bacchus and a sinuous Bacchante framed by an overturned drinker and a piper. This filling of the picture plane with figures, this *horror vacui*, reveals a certain indifference to the pictorial value of space and a preference for forms viewed from close up.

A linocut on the same theme (reproduced on the title page) serves very well to illustrate the way in which a technique succeeds in transforming a subject. Whereas wash drawing is highly suitable for painterly modulations, the linocut—Picasso has called it the "most artisan and least refined" of all engraving procedures—incites the artist to summary notations. In a conventional landscape the faun playing the pipe and the couple composed of satyr and nymph (reduced to a sort of amoeboid squiggle) are set like the reference points we expect to see in any bacchanal under the immense drapery of a sky adorned with sumptuous white embroidery suspended from the clouds as from enormous nails. In this graphic fantasy the allurements of a technique whose sobriety recalls the woodcut become the vehicle of poetry. The Greek idyll, simplified to the point where it is but the transparent symbol of itself, is admitted in its own right to the museum of the twentieth century.

Like chamber music that must be listened to for its own sake, Picasso's drawings evade the limitations of book illustration. They express his wit, his obsessions, his longings, his deep-seated love of play, in absolute freedom with a pen or brush that ignores the fixity of painted or sculptured signs and reflects the mobility of an elusive temperament.

THE PERMANENCE OF CUBISM

[To say that] Picasso enters and leaves Cubism as one
enters and leaves a country house each summer...
makes no more sense than to say that Renoir enters
and leaves Impressionism.

PIERRE FRANCASTEL

WHERE are all those café tables that were chopped up and put
together again during the "heroic years"? It would be vain
to search for their equivalent from 1950 to 1968. *Two Women on
the Beach* recalls the Cubism of *Les Demoiselles d'Avignon* rather
than that of the guitars and bottles of Bass.

When Léger said that "the quality of a pictorial work is in
direct proportion to its *quantity of realism*" and spoke of the
"state of organized plastic intensity," he gave a perfect definition
of the character of Cubist "realism," which had ceased to be
imitative and had become quantitative-intensive.

In *Woman with a Dog* we find a painting that is explicitly "in
movement," but the movement is not so much expressed as
stated in the compensated imbalance of two static forms. The
impression we receive is rather like that of a snapshot, an impression of congealed movement. In fact, this static quality seems
to be an indispensable factor in the coherence of the system.
Once it has rejected *in toto* the tricks of the image, it is hard for
us to see why Cubism should have retained the illusion of movement after eliminating the illusion of depth: each constitutes a
different aspect of the illusion of reality. Cubist logic requires
the painter to depict objects in a "flat, colored architecture," not
as he sees them but as they are made.

One cannot overstate the point to which Picasso pushed his
challenge to the traditional system, not only in its forms but
also in its economy, its operation, its aesthetic. For hundreds of

WOMAN WITH A DOG, MARCH 8, 1953. OIL.

The firm design, the patches of color laid absolutely flat on the canvas, the counterpoint (which since the *Milliner's Workshop* of 1926 has simplified traditional chiaroscuro and distributed light areas and dark solely with a view to ensuring plastic balance), together with the elimination of all movement that "disarranges the lines," recreate the appearance of classic Cubist painting. "For me," says Picasso, "the role of painting is not to paint movement... but rather to stop movement."

This picture, a stereometric construction of two women-objects, might be a sketch for a sculpture in sheet iron. The massive bulk of the bodies that carry effortlessly their flattened insect heads, the hugeness of the feet whose purpose is to anchor the bodies to the ground, the upright posture of the figure on the left, the heavy curvature of the one on the right, reveal a concern for solidity that is one of the constants of Cubism. The half-ironic allusion to the classic theme of "Women at their Toilet" stresses the absence, in this poetic construction, of any immediate social reference.

TWO WOMEN ON THE BEACH, FEBRUARY 16, 1956. OIL.

years painters had exploited, with increasing ingenuity, the propensity of the image for the pretences of illusionism. The spectator's eye, an accomplice before the fact, passed through that virtual looking-glass, the canvas, and entered the artificial paradise of a reflex-space, a dream-space. Whether in terms of myth, allegory or sentiment, painting provided the means to attain a cultural scene, a vision of the world, for which it was only partly responsible.

WOMAN UNDER A PINE TREE, JANUARY 20, 1959. OIL.

A Cubist work, instead, creates a break-away poetry. The techniques employed with that end in view—the broken line, the figure divorced from the background, the double profile—produce an effect of discontinuity that is not exclusively physical. As a side effect we find a *cultural break-away*, which perhaps explains why Cubism is regarded without comprehension but also without hostility.

This is also true of *Woman under a Pine Tree*, a "sculptured" form that fills the entire canvas as if Picasso was obsessed by what he calls "the void between the frame and the picture." There are painters of space, for instance Cézanne and Matisse; Picasso is a painter of objects. Objects viewed from close up and perceived as volumes. In this young giantess, who reminds us less of Baudelaire than of Gulliver, the female nude becomes a colossal geography. This close-up vision must seem monstrous to anyone who has remained true to the exclusive criteria of optical painting. But if one is willing to admit that here the sense of sight acts as a go-between for the sense of touch and to apprehend the form from within, so to say, taking as reference point the perception of one's own body, one is far less scandalized by this huge sculptured sign. The succession of volumes, conjuring up a structure in concrete cut up by the interplay of light and shade, is a plastic transposition of the passive heaviness of a siesta which the spectator himself is invited to share.

This brings us to the end of a development that started with the *Demoiselles d'Avignon* and the Negro period, when Cubism had not yet utilized the decomposition of the planes. Picasso has reverted periodically to this Cubism of volumes, this opaque plasticism that completely excludes dreams, except perhaps the daydreams that Gaston Bachelard said were linked with the "earth." The nude is a first-class test of an artist's intentions. Face to face with this one, we cannot but recall Léger's decisive dictum: "We realized that melody was done for."

THE STUDIO, LA CALIFORNIE, APRIL 2, 1956. OIL.

The Art Nouveau frame of the window of the dark studio is silhouetted against a harsh light that reveals a jumble of easels and canvases, the brightly lighted corner of a wall, a samovar, a lozenge-shaped sculpture placed on a table. Here Matisse's delicate color harmonies give way to a stern "Spanish" chiaroscuro based on three tone-values, whose sobriety contrasts with the bright Riviera colors of other variations on the same theme in which we can see the palm trees through the window.

"LA CALIFORNIE"

Towards the end of 1955 Picasso moved to Cannes, where he took up his abode in "La Californie," a typical Riviera villa in the style of 1900. That outmoded Art Nouveau style has not yet come back into fashion. But how could Picasso, who has always been sensitive to local atmosphere, remain indifferent to the anachronism of his new home?

For close on a year he painted a series of *Studios* in which, for the first time, the environment seems to be more important than the human beings situated in it. Maybe he recalled Matisse, who treated with rare felicity the theme of the "interior" which was so well suited to his euphoric art.

A little of his joy pervades the many pictures of La Californie, whether enlivened or not by the presence of Jacqueline. In some she is painted in Turkish costume: "Matisse is dead," said Picasso, "and has left me his Odalisques." But that is as far as the resemblance goes. Matisse's values—except perhaps in one of the very first canvases, painted the same day (October 23, 1955) in a second version that is already decidedly Picassian—must undergo a transmutation before they can gain admittance to Picasso's world.

In others the motley coloring of the Riviera, the green of the palm trees, the brilliant yellow of sun and walls, encroaches on the bric-à-brac of the villa-studio. In all—and there is nothing strange in that—Picasso is at pains to express forms: the arabesque of the Art Nouveau window-frame is the leitmotiv that

SPRING, LA CALIFORNIE, MARCH 20, 1956. OIL.

links the rocking chair, the palm trees, the litter in the studio, and at times the "baroque" ornamentation of walls and ceiling.

In each of the three different series that one can distinguish in the 1955-1956 period, Picasso tended towards a more and more radical simplification, ending up with fragmented, schematic designs based on straight lines. But even more remarkable than the development of the execution is that of the various themes.

The chronology of that period—Picasso had long been accustomed to date his works with the day and the month—proves that the theme of the "empty studio" held his interest for a very short time. Almost immediately the human figure asserted its tyrannical presence in the versions of *Woman in Turkish Costume*, a dynamic portrait of Jacqueline Picasso, and after it in a series of nudes and seated women. Conversely, the "empty studio," which at the outset laid claim to large canvases, found the space at its disposal progressively curtailed and soon gave way to the "woman in the studio" theme. It is the old theme of the Painter and his Model but the Painter is missing.

What this evolution involved is clear to see: Picasso very soon abandoned the general view of what he called "studio landscapes" and adopted a close-up viewpoint which enabled him to see not only the space but the beings and objects that occupy it. This imperceptible shift from the angle of landscape to that of portrait and still life is one of the constants of Cubist realism and of Picasso's art. In the end the handwriting of forms prevailed over the global expression of space because space is what one cannot touch.

VAUVENARGUES
OR THE RETURN TO PAINTING
1959-1961

WHEN Picasso moved into the château of Vauvenargues in 1959 a friend of his warned him against its melancholy atmosphere. The artist replied that "he was not afraid of that because he was a Spaniard." As a matter of fact, he seems to have found at Vauvenargues what Maurice Jardot called "an entirely inward Spain, ardent and grave, a Spain of the depths." It was there that he copied Murillo's *El Bobo* and once again reverted to the bullfight with the important Picador series.

A new setting inspired new themes. More important still, and a frequent occurrence with Picasso, the change of place led to a change of style, which on this occasion seems to have been even more drastic than usual. In fact, the works produced during the two years Picasso lived at Vauvenargues initiated a return to color.

The use of enamel paint has been so much more frequent during this late period that it has come to be one of its characteristic traits. Was this one of the reasons for Picasso's renewed interest in color? Be that as it may, in one of the major works of the period, *The Dining Room at Vauvenargues*, he made full use of industrial lacquer's capacity of spreading over broad, frayed areas of color. Was it perhaps the fact of liberally abandoning the initiative to the material substance of the paint that baffled the public in the last rooms of the Grand Palais, at the Homage to Picasso exhibition, by revealing the existence of another, unknown Picasso? A technique in which the pictorial "unit"

THE DINING ROOM AT VAUVENARGUES,
MARCH 23, 1959/JANUARY 23, 1960. OIL.

A huge Renaissance sideboard dominates the center of the composition,
swallowing up the silhouette of a table and the black head of the dog,
whose body stands out in vivid white blotches. These direct light effects
and the child's face, which is reduced to a featureless grey blot, justify
us in speaking of a "return to painting." In his corrections on the right-
hand side of the picture—they can be clearly seen in the original—Picasso
blotted out one whole section of his initial composition with white paint,
stressing very sharply the lateral outline of the sideboard and "reserving"
the silhouette of a sort of female bust.

is not the line or dab of paint but the patch or pool of color, tends naturally to exclude effects of volume, which are dependent rather on firm contours. In accordance with a logic which in ultimate analysis is the logic of the material, objects and figures are specified on the picture plane as a juxtaposition of silhouettes.

The use of black suggested by the somber aspect of the Renaissance sideboard enhances the general impression of objects viewed against the light. The peculiarly painterly interest of these blacks heightened with violets and greens and enlivened by the reds of the floor is a sufficiently rare occurrence in Picasso's work to warrant special mention. (If one masks the reds, the violets and greens seem to fade into a delicate harmony of cold tones.) Picasso often uses color merely as a means to facilitate the reading of the forms and double their assault; here instead consonances and dissonances seem to obey the law of complementaries (orange/green) or the rule that cold tones (blue, violet, emerald green) recede while warm tones (orange, vermilion) advance. The play of the color patches—they are large enough to act as forms in their own right—makes this sideboard of Vauvenargues a very fine piece of pure painting: in fact, Figuration can contain its own Abstraction.

The return to color takes another shape in the still lifes painted at Vauvenargues. Here are two different versions of the same theme, *Mandolin, Jug and Glass*, in which the jug is embellished with a schematic emblem that resembles a little dancing faun. The objects are vigorously outlined or clearly defined by their shadows in a ternary composition that occurs quite frequently in Picasso. The color scheme is reduced to three primary colors: red and yellow patches on a severe, rustic bottle green. What is new is the fact that, freed from the supremacy of the form, the colors spread beyond the objects as in some works by Léger and Chagall. The objects group themselves in total freedom. "I put into my painting everything I love. So much the worse for the objects! They must agree among themselves." In the second version the background is enlivened with parallel lines that form waves around the contours of the objects (the handle of the jug, the keys of the mandolin). Is it the object that invades space or space that encroaches on the object?

MANDOLIN, JUG AND GLASS, APRIL 11, 1959, IV. OIL.

MANDOLIN, JUG AND GLASS, APRIL 16, 1959/MAY 5, 1959, III. OIL.

In any case, even a space that is no longer a bottomless void
reveals a painter's preoccupation. Though here, in truth, the
painter considers himself closer to the motley colors of folk
art than to a learned tradition intent on rendering every detail
of aerial perspective.

WOMAN WITH CLASPED HANDS, APRIL 28, 1959, III. OIL.

A *Woman with Clasped Hands*, also painted at Vauvenargues, bears witness to the permanence of the cruel handwriting of the terrible "seated women," who are far from being exclusive phenomena of the war years. In this head, which is shifted towards the right by a bun of hair, face and profile are superposed rather than juxtaposed; in fact, a face heavily outlined in black is painted over the light-colored, sharp-nosed profile. As in some very early portraits (of Dora Maar), Picasso has stressed the eyes by situating them on the edge of the form. (The "arbitrary" lines that link the ears with the center of the face do not render something we can actually see but express a tension.)

"Distortion," says Jean Cassou, "is for him a stylistic, intellectual procedure that ended up by satisfying a more obscure, essentially Spanish taste: the taste for monsters." But how does one recognize a monster? "Oh yes! Of course, a sheep with five feet," said an inhabitant of Vallauris of *Man with a Sheep*, though he was in a position to see for himself every day that Picasso's sheep have only four feet. His words not only define the sole indisputable criterion for judging monstrosity —the criterion of biology—they prove that after all monstrosity is wherever we want to put it. As a matter of fact, except for a very few Surrealist drawings he did in the 1930s and a few admitted monsters, Picasso has only transgressed the biological norm in the proportions of his figures. We must distinguish between what is explicitly monstrous and a freely constructed sign, namely a collection of distinctive elements that may be rendered with a wide margin of discretion on condition that they remain easily identifiable. This head doesn't seem monstrous if we stop looking at it as an "image." It is expressive and nothing more. In the same way as handwriting or an African mask. An expression of this sort, based on the most absolute impenetrability and impossible to render in words is a very cogent example of poetic ambivalence.

INFANTA, SEPTEMBER 14, 1957. OIL.

TERRORISTIC ARCHAEOLOGY

What is a painter? He is a collector who forms
a collection by making his own paintings of
the pictures he finds to his liking in other
people's homes.

PICASSO

WHETHER it is due to an elementary mimetism or to a
striving for identification, a pastiche always makes the
work it took as its model the Alpha and Omega of a search for
knowledge, not of an act of creation. Picasso follows an inverse
procedure in his "copies" of other masters. Cézanne used to go
to the Louvre to "do Poussin over again after nature"; Picasso,
instead, copied *Las Meninas* to do "after Velazquez" Picassos he
had not yet conceived. Hence his attitude towards the master-
pieces of other artists is only apparently disrespectful. Picasso
copies solely what he admires and never produces a parody.
What he does is simply to treat as a "natural phenomenon"
something that has already been elaborated by art.

In this *Portrait of a Painter* after El Greco, Picasso says he
endeavored to render the Spanish master's "lunar light." We
should not be surprised that he did so by a simplification and
radicalization of effects which matches his temperament no less
closely than it matches Cubist procedures. We note, for instance,
in the highlights on the faces that El Greco's modelling (which
is relatively harsh compared with the customary technique of
his day) is rendered by Picasso with contrasts that are still
sharper. The transition from light to shade, which classical
painters strove to render imperceptible, is replaced by hard
outlines that carve the form into planes which are alternately
light and dark. Even the reflex highlights on brow, lips and chin
have become curious little disks outlined in black. Once we have

accepted the usual Cubist convention of the division of space, this is "the most natural way to say things," to use Picasso's words. Whereas the lace collar and cuffs have undergone a geometrical simplification, the hand holding the brush is treated as an expressive arabesque. The profile (turned towards the left) has preserved, as if in jest, a "period" character. Light, elegance, historical color, everything barely hinted at in El Greco's subtle image has been transformed into explicit signs.

The version of *The Women of Algiers* reproduced here is the last of the fifteen paintings executed between December 13, 1954, and February 14, 1955. Picasso has completely transformed

EL GRECO: PORTRAIT OF A PAINTER, 1600-1604.

PORTRAIT OF A PAINTER AFTER EL GRECO, FEBRUARY 22, 1950. OIL ON WOOD.

Delacroix's picture, sacrificing unity to his passion for contrast and the Romantic master's chiaroscuro effects to a brilliant color scheme. The first two versions of the series are couched in admirable arabesques whose suppleness reminds one of Matisse. In the third, executed a fortnight later, the position of the two principal figures has been changed completely, in line with a trend that is still more strongly marked in the following variations on the same theme. The quasi-parallelism, which in Delacroix might suggest the idea of a friendship between two inmates of the harem, has been replaced by Picasso with a drastic contrast. The woman with the narghile, who wears an oriental négligé, is congealed in a serene verticality; her companion is no longer seated but lies with her feet resting on a small hexagonal table. The servant girl taking out the coffee tray forms a dance figure, which is the only movement in this static evocation of oriental repose. In the place of Delacroix's

DELACROIX: THE WOMEN OF ALGIERS, 1834.

THE WOMEN OF ALGIERS AFTER DELACROIX, FEBRUARY 14, 1955. OIL.

Despite its exoticism, Delacroix's painting was all delicate transitions. Here, instead, the contrasting postures are stressed by the contrasted handling. The woman with the narghile is treated in the colorful style of peasant embroidery, in which the design evokes popular prints. Instead, the two figures on the right (and a third which is framed by the open doorway) present a play of alternating Cubist signs and planes. The contrast is so sharp that the figure on the left seems to occupy a marginal position.

unobtrusively local color and mild eroticism, Picasso has given us a construction in which the picturesque is concentrated in a few signs and the erotic expands all the more freely now that realism interests him no longer.

Twenty years before he painted the Meninas series, Picasso said of Velazquez: "This is still better than Le Nain. *Las Meninas*, what a picture! Here we have the true painter of reality!" In this work, astonishing in its modernism, Velazquez portrayed himself in his capacity as court painter, while the image of his royal patron is but a pale reflection in the depths of a looking-glass. The spectator occupies the place of the model

VELAZQUEZ: LAS MENINAS (THE MAIDS OF HONOR), 1656.

LAS MENINAS AFTER VELAZQUEZ, AUGUST 17, 1957. OIL.

As in *The Women of Algiers*, the handwriting becomes more and more elliptical as we read the picture from left to right (cf. the sullen dwarf, the uncertain arabesque of the page). Here there is no question of Cubism but of a handling inspired by children's drawings (as is confirmed by other versions of the same series). It is not that Picasso wanted to suit his handwriting to the subject, but simply that his own children, Claude and Paloma, had reached the age when children draw. Could that impassioned inventor of signs fail to be interested in the infantile drawing that creates signs which are perhaps all the purer for their clumsiness?

and is asked to contemplate not the conventional space in which the model holds a pose, but the space of real life with children, maids in waiting, pages playing with their pets, and a nobleman seen against the light as he withdraws through a half-open door.

Picasso made no attempt to imitate the technique used by Velazquez (so he was quite content to do without the actual presence of the original) or to capt a message that may well have seemed rather unusual at the Spanish court. In one of the variants the accent is placed on the looking-glass, whose forms irradiate the entire picture in an interplay of dovetailed planes reflected to infinity—a plastic transposition of what has been termed, in a definition of classical western art, the "aesthetic of the mirror." Here, instead, the figure of the painter, wearing a cloak adorned with the Grand Cross of the Order of Santiago, is restored to the pre-eminence it enjoyed in the original.

MANET: LE DÉJEUNER SUR L'HERBE, 1863.

LE DÉJEUNER SUR L'HERBE AFTER MANET, MARCH 3, 1960/
AUGUST 20, 1960. OIL.

Picasso has used means different from but no less effective than Manet's
to suggest the green and blue thickets of this picnic site, from which the
silhouettes of the two bathers and the two art students emerge in a play
of light and shade. The ochres and browns mixed with the green of the
seated bather recall the apparent disorder of a burgeoning vegetation, which
is repeated in the vermiculated embroidery of the foliage. This in no way
excludes the exact placing of the figures in space. The composition gives
rise to a discontinuous assemblage of signs, each of which occupies the
place allotted to it once and for all. Here we find the conventions of archaic
pictorial narrative, in bas-relief and mosaic, in miniature and fresco.

There is no fundamental difference between these variations on a famous masterpiece and the works for which Picasso found his inspiration in reality. But the divergence of the copy from the original pinpoints the path that leads to intense expression, as in this study of an Infanta which is bereft of the least trace of illusionism. It is a creation at one remove. Delacroix used to say that he would be glad to spend his life "matching the Ways of the Cross in village churches." Picasso told Hélène Parmelin that "sometimes one is freest just when one thinks one is least free. And not at all when you feel you have a giant's wings that prevent your walking a step."

From February 1960 to August 1961 Picasso did a series of 27 paintings and 138 drawings, nearly all of them at Mougins, that deserves a place of its own on account of its size. In these *Déjeuners* it is thrilling to see how he transposes the art that was most alien to his temperament: Impressionism. Manet's picture may not be a typical Impressionist landscape, but it does offer us a natural space that lends itself uneasily to the geometrical simplifications of which Picasso was so fond. The version reproduced here—it is the fifth of the series and the painter worked on it off and on over a period of six months—proves that he had no intention of evading difficulty by sacrificing once again "the space between the frame and the picture," the three-dimensional space in which the figures are immersed. This makes it perhaps the picture in which Picasso is closest to a landscape painter. One is struck by the painterly richness, the peculiar vibration, the exquisite medley of sensations that are undoubtedly the basis of the pleasure we find in colorism and in all painting of light.

What shocked critics and public in 1863, who were seemingly not much impressed by Manet's reference to Giorgione's *Concert champêtre*, was no doubt the nonchalance of the two men who carried on their conversation without feeling in the least embarrassed by the scandalous presence of a nude woman whose absolute naturalness contrasted with a studied composition that wanted to appear improvised. Picasso eliminated this allusive, anecdotic aspect and replaced it with a hieratic style that emphasizes the forms. In another version, as in the whole long series of drawings, one is struck by the perfect legibility of the composition. As in a medieval fresco or a Byzantine mosaic, each important figure is enclosed in an unbroken contour.

Here we find once again the tendency towards colorism that already appeared in the pictures Picasso painted a little earlier at Vauvenargues, where he had in fact started work on several versions of the *Déjeuner*. But we also find the same unwillingness to revert to the most inimitable and personal qualities of the brushwork. Aragon said that "in the past a painter was linked with his picture by a mysterious physical relationship similar to that between father and son." Picasso broke that equivocal bond. The transposition of an Impressionist painting would have warranted, more than any other, his resorting to the inimitable handling he had used himself in his blue and rose periods. But that would have implied reverting to a tradition he had definitively condemned since the *Demoiselles d'Avignon*.

Picasso succeeded nonetheless in rendering even the Impressionist technique "readable" to a certain extent in this splendid version. The impalpable something which is Manet's "manner" is transcribed in a painterly texture that is no longer inimitable but is made up of identifiable elements and calligraphic conventions. Thus the foliage that dominates the whole picture is represented by rows of dots and fringes, by contours festooned with commas (for instance, around the heads of the two main figures, where the space recedes as if the better to frame the forms). The figure of the bather is rendered with elongated bulbosities bounded by outlines that vary in thickness to express the parts in full sunlight and the areas of shadow. These conventions give the whole picture a stylistic unity that existed in a

THE RAPE OF THE SABINE WOMEN AFTER DAVID, JANUARY 9, 1963/
FEBRUARY 7, 1963. OIL.

diffuse, intangible state in Manet's work. That mysterious factor of painting, the handling, has undergone a transmutation which makes it one of the explicit "forms" of the work. "In a modern painting," Picasso told Cocteau, "every stroke is a precision job."

In his version of David's *Rape of the Sabine Women*, academic handwriting has undergone a transposition affecting both space and figures. On the one hand we find a pseudo-illusionistic space just as flat as Uccello's. On the other hand the signs inscribed in that space are summarily dressed up as images thanks to pseudo-modelling, pseudo-local tone and pseudo-highlights. The pictorial illusion is "simulated," in turn, but this simulation at one remove gives the game away.

The historical panoply dear to David has been reduced to a few conventional props—helmet and buckler, sword and temple. This has the additional advantage of putting the anecdote in the background and bringing out the permanent significance of the theme, namely the struggle for the conquest of woman. If there is any truth at all in academicism, it lies undoubtedly in its preference for universal values. But if the message is to reach us it must not get bogged down in superflous erudition and the empty chit-chat of the image. "One must know how to be vulgar," says Picasso, whose shrill figuration has ousted David's frigid distinction. With Picasso, the art of the past becomes the object of terroristic archaeological research.

In this *Rape of the Sabine Women*, Picasso has paradoxically kept David's rhetoric: a very explicit composition in two registers, one above the other; and gestures of remarkable eloquence (warriors with blazing eyes thrusting at each other; screaming children; women in disordered attire). But simplified conventions and vigorous accents enliven the coldness of the original. Here the psychological detachment normally achieved by pushing back the spectacle in space is abolished by the closely packed figures. Artificially crowded together, these fill virtually the entire surface of the canvas. It is not by chance that the scenic background is only glimpsed here and there.

THE PAINTER AND HIS MODEL, APRIL 2-6, 1963. OIL.

The studied technique of brushstroke and modelling is deliberately replaced by a system of daubs, as in the handling of the Painter's hat, hand and foot. The careful distribution of the highlights in a traditional nude has given place to a mere cut-out in which the crudely treated background leaves vacant the blank space occupied by the white silhouette. "What I am looking for just now," Picasso told Hélène Parmelin, "is the word that will say 'nude' on my canvas, at one stroke, without any fuss... Here at first glance the nude makes no bones about telling you what it is." This "gigantic pictogram" is Picasso's version of Art in the raw, but it does not indulge in the pathological or in what Renato Barilli, speaking of Dubuffet, termed "regressive figuration." Rather is it a question here of "childhood recovered at will" (Baudelaire).

"THE PAINTER AND HIS MODEL"
OR STYLE CALLED IN QUESTION

Art production is a field given over
to the spirit of caprice.

JEAN DUBUFFET

THE Painter and His Model and Seated Nude Woman are two typical examples of figurative art in Picasso's œuvre. But there are times when, as a supreme irony, the Painter takes both easel and model "into the open." Then he gives us a semi-satirical account of a nap after a picnic entitled *Sleeping Couple,* the unexpected theme of the *Watermelon Eaters,* or the well-known theme of the Bather on the Beach.

If we find these works baffling it is because they offer us a painting which, in its effort to divest itself of "style," frankly feigns technical clumsiness. "Technique is all right," says Picasso, "if one has so much of it that it ceases to exist." That is a wager he laid and won. Here are some works that parade the procedures of traditional painting—brushstrokes and patches, even modelling—but magnify them to the point of absurdity, to the point where they have been deliberately given the appearance of paintings done by children. The illusionistic technique has been demystified by taking it absolutely at its face value. By virtue of the modern ethic that no longer demands the naïve sincerity of the content but transparent intentions and technical honesty, once a procedure has been *admitted* and evades illusionistic trickery it becomes perfectly *admissible.*

Picasso, who at the age of twelve "drew like Raphael," confesses that it took him a long time to learn to paint "like a child." Here in fact the rule—there is a rule in everything Picasso does—seems to be that the forms must not be a pretext

WATERMELON EATERS AND CHICKEN, APRIL 19, 1965, II. OIL.

for the execution but must arise out of the daubs themselves just as they do in a *real* child's painting (observe the hands and feet of the female melon eater).

During his Cubist period, criticism and analysis were focused on the *planes*, the structural elements of the picture. Today they are focused on the *handling*. On the other hand, the composition is less naïve than it seems: might not the diagonal marked by the cock and the slice of melon perhaps represent, in this juicy painting, a sort of Freudian transfer of desire?

In *Seated Nude Woman* the way in which the legs are treated offers ample confirmation of this rejection of style by deliberately

SEATED NUDE WOMAN, JANUARY 7, 1965, II. OIL.

clumsy handling. The archaic elegance of the design frames in a scroll of dark dots a face that is vaguely reminiscent of Coptic art or the Fayum.

Is Picasso simply "having a little fun" or does he want to prove that one can make a work of art with anything and everything? With the most hackneyed technique, the coarsest handling, the vaguest borrowings, but only if one uses them to produce forms: for forms are the perceptible and, so to say, ponderable elements of that half-instinctive, half-conscious construction—a work of art. In the past bits of rubbish were pressed into the service of art; now an apparent absence of technique is employed for the same purpose without losing its spontaneity. The result is daring works of an art that has a masterly naïvety and is the perfect illustration of what André Breton meant when he said: "The eye exists in the wild state."

AFTER the first exhibition of his ceramics in the Maison de la Pensée Française in 1946 Picasso said: "They are disappointed if the monster merely smiles." But one has only to compare the ceramics in the Musée Grimaldi at Antibes with the well-meaning researches of forms and materials assembled at Vallauris in 1968 for the First International Biennale of Ceramics to realize the amazing vitality of Picasso's creations in this field. They possess exactly what is lacking in the products of the ablest craftsmen. They have the same love of the material and feeling for it and in addition display a fluent design that controls the form.

The decoration is not limited to the surface of the object: it pervades it and brings it to life. Everyone knows the famous dishes with bullfight scenes in which the form suggests the composition of the subject: the flat of the dish represents the bullring, its edge the tiers of seats crowded with spectators. There are others in which the flat becomes the sun's face or a faun's head and the design is all the more preponderant in that it started by accepting the form of the object.

The harmony is perfect when the decoration, the form-image, is identical with the form-function, as in the famous vase-women that lie midway between pottery and sculpture. In some of them the form turned on the potter's wheel represents the curves of the female figure. Others—this one, for instance—display a simple head, round and naïve, with a rustic

OWL, 1956. RED TERRACOTTA.

bouquet in the hair, midway between an eighteenth-century pastoral and a Munich beer cellar. In the same way, when Picasso produced his *Doves* at Vallauris, he rejected the classic method of modelling, which consists in pressing lumps of clay with the thumb. He preferred to study the age-old movements of the professional potters in the workshop of Georges and Suzanne Ramié. Fascinated by the half-finished forms that the potter gives the clay, he took frits or rough forms (still soft after drying for one day) and treated them as one would a piece of cloth that was capable of being folded, creased, crumpled, stuck to itself. Without any attempt at illusion on his part, under the pressure of his fingers the ductile substance spontaneously imitates the forms of life.

DOVE AND FLOWER-CROWNED WOMAN'S HEAD, OCTOBER 14, 1950 AND MARCH 20, 1954. CERAMICS.

At times the result is still more in keeping with his gift for intense, instantaneous expression. On the red terracotta of this Provençal tile the rudimental sign of an owl bursts forth in black and white. If the lower pattern serves merely as a support for the design, the upper one suggests the night-bird's huddled head and the starting point of the wings: sign and object are one. The unexpected appearance of the roughly marked lump of clay frees it from the fetters of a commonplace language. An acute sense of droll inventiveness makes the oldest of the arts of fire stir with a tremor of youth.

FORMS IN THE CITY

Painting is not made for decorating apartments.

W HEREAS Calder likes to take advantage of the industrial aspect of a material, Picasso cuts his sheet iron with the sensibility of a craftsman. We can see this in the "folded and painted sheet iron" that represents in white on black a *Woman with Outstretched Arms*.

Long before 1960 Picasso had taken an interest in creating on an urban scale. Between 1927 and 1929 he toyed with the idea of erecting on the Croisette at Cannes apartment houses in the form of sculptures—"monuments" representing greatly distorted Bathers; but they never got beyond the stage of drawings or paintings. "I have to paint them," he used to say with the ghost of a smile, "because I'm not allowed to build them." Picasso never missed an opportunity—whether in *Guernica*, his four big stage curtains, the immense panel for UNESCO, the *Temple of Peace*, or these late sculptures—to work on large surfaces, for he was convinced that painting and sculpture are not made "for decorating apartments." It is not that he always wanted to proclaim in that way, by sheer size, his "lofty sentiments" and ideological commitment. But an art that relinquishes the lure of a subjective vision in favor of intense forms and universal signs was less able than any other to accept the strictures of reduced scale.

Monumental scale is a pitiless test! Can you imagine Dadaist or Surrealist works or the vast majority of abstract works leaving the apartments they embellish and accepting the challenge

WOMAN WITH OUTSTRETCHED ARMS, CANNES, 1961.
SHEET IRON CUT, FOLDED AND PAINTED.

of the street? Purely cerebral subversion and artificial paradises cannot stand up to the scale of a big modern building. What brute size kills is not the subject of the work but its inwardness. Perhaps it only suffers works that possess an extreme plastic rigor, in which Form, Line, Material and Color are the indispensable factors. Painting based on handling is dead. On the industrial scale, only large-sized signs can survive.

Nonetheless, when an artist lays aside the paintbrush in favor of new materials, that does not exempt him from the duty to recover through their novel aspects his feeling for the material, which is an indispensable element of a work. Modern industry thrusts upon an artist who works on a monumental scale media more elemental than those employed by traditional craftsmen and at the same time demands still more feeling for them. Line in particular, which is the purest and most impalpable of all media, finds its value greatly enhanced by mere size. Today, as in archaic times, every great artist is both draughtsman and sculptor. That, no doubt, is one of the most deep-rooted reasons for Picasso's supremacy.

A novel technique called "bétograve" or sanded concrete has been invented seemingly for the sole purpose of making that supremacy more obvious, as if such a thing were necessary.

The anthropological generality of the sign, which is simplified in the extreme, is economically stressed by the clear, yet abstract indication of the sex and by a few stray commas which seem to say that there is no point in complying with the conventional stenography of the face. On the other hand, the slightly curved outlines and the sharp fold that bends one arm backwards attest the rapid, definitive decision, the elegant, untrammelled freedom indispensable in a cut-out. The blank whiteness of the surfaces would recall the flexibility of a paper model were it not accompanied by a close mesh in glossy black that stresses the rigidity of metal. It is worth noting that the monumental effect is enhanced by the broadening of the hands and feet, in contrast to the punctiform head.

It was developed by the Norwegian painter and sculptor, Karl Nesjar, and consists in casting, in a mold that reproduces the overall shape of the work, a white concrete which contains an aggregate of gravel or crushed stones. "Owing to the difference in density between the various constituent elements," Pierre Gascar tells us, "any sort of concrete has a surface where the cement that acts as a binder is slightly more in evidence than in the depths of the mass. This is what has led masons and architects to talk about the 'skin of the concrete'... When the concrete is scoured with a high-pressure sand blast it reveals the color and grain of the aggregate of which it is made." The artist can cut a linear furrow of greater or lesser depth or, "by corroding more or less the skin of the concrete, reveal clearly or vaguely the sort of sedimentary deposit represented by the heart of the concrete and establish over vast areas contrasts of values, colors and textures."

This technique has obvious affinities with the Cubist aesthetic. The constraints imposed by the mold and the relative uniformity of the aggregate demand ample forms enclosed in straight lines or simple curves and bar over-complex effects of color. On the other hand the procedure reproduces every detail of the design and even the grain of the material, thus eluding the coldness generally attributed to concrete. Picasso met Karl Nesjar in 1956 and since then has taken a great interest in this technique. He used it for several models that were on show in the Petit Palais in 1966-1967. They represent "cut-out figures," "folded" sculptures or posts that support a head projected on two planes which intersect at right angles, like an immobilized weather-cock or a "signal" that sends out the simplest of human messages to the four corners of the globe. Since 1956 a dozen of these works have been executed in concrete and set up in Oslo (1956); in the College of Architects, Barcelona (1961); on the lake shore at Khristinehamn, Sweden (1965); in the Lycée

WOMAN'S HEAD, 1965. CONCRETE.

Sud, Marseilles, and in the Museum of Modern Art, Stockholm (1965). Should we accept Michel Ragon's prophecy that "a fabulous prospect awaits future painters: whole towns to paint"?

We can at least dream of a townscape where, amid the geometrical constructions that are no doubt inevitable, these aerial paintings will alleviate the planned tedium of the suburbs and their huge blocks of flats or enliven the dullness of the traffic beacons by installing their blinking lights in the round eyes of certain "heads." The comparison with some abstract signals that already rear their huge metal hulks skywards would help figurative works to make their impact felt and recover all their virulence. Setting the motley seal of a heretical irony here and there on the vast expanse of white stereometry, these gigantic colored signposts would attest that life interferes obstinately, gratuitously and unseasonably with the logic of town planners.

THE VOYAGE OF THE YOUNG ANACHARSIS

E VERYTHING was definitively cut and dried, or so it seemed.
After a tender prologue in blue and rose, the harsh oeuvre
continued to make its dreadful cries heard in a world peopled
by phantoms—Pompeian, Hellenistic, Iberian, Etruscan—that
mimicked the procedures of an ancient art and endowed it with
a youth it had "long forgotten or perhaps never actually pos-
sessed." Interludes lulled our expectation with new monsters or
a delightful composite ballet: dancers passing to and fro with
a hint of their traditional gestures, harlequins dreaming with
their masks in their hands, fauns pursuing nymphs, children
playing amid innumerable seated or recumbent women, old men
in contemplation; a blind Minotaur prowling, tortured and terrible. Even in this theater of the unexpected it was hard to imagine new surprises. But Picasso, regardless of the official honors
showered upon him on the occasion of the "Homage" shows,
went on working as usual. In 1968 the public was summoned
to view some large drawings: as usual what they saw was not
what they had expected.

This time it was the voyage of a Young Anacharsis eighty-
five years of age through an Odyssean, anachronistic Mediterranean where musketeers in plumed hats and painters wearing
the ruffs and rapiers of Spanish grandees mingle in bucolic
siestas accompanied by fauns playing their pipes, Penelopes
decked out to welcome the returning warrior, Ledas dreaming
of swans—age-old myths travestied beyond recognition.

MYTHOLOGICAL SCENE, AUGUST 30, 1967. PENCIL.

Wearing a broad-brimmed Greek hat in intricately plaited straw, the Peasant, Messenger or Squire precedes the Warrior who enters on a chariot adorned with a monster intended to strike terror into the enemy. Penelope, bejewelled and marcelled, with made-up eye and painted nails, awaits him. One is surprised to see, close beside the mythical woman and apparently under her protection, a wrinkled little old man dressed as a musketeer and holding a stout cudgel in his enormous hands, who seems to represent a "donor" or a "voyeur." A far from sacred mythology, to match the Greece that invented the "smile of the gods."

This evocative, incongruous and anachronistic trio, *Faun, Nude Woman and Musketeer*, brings the series to a close. On the left a Faun, abundantly hairy and horned, waits with an impatience that Picasso's pencil seemingly decided to veil at the very last moment. On the right a Musketeer, bewigged and in full fig, carries the plume and pike that are the symbolic weapons of all sane strategy. The ill-assorted pair are pressing their attentions on a far from bashful nymph, whose suggestive posture and tender gaze show that she has no intention of discouraging either the antique swain or the more urbane suitor. An eroticism that has nothing in common with Sade.

FAUN, NUDE WOMAN AND MUSKETEER, SEPTEMBER 6, 1967. DRAWING.

The cycle unfolds in "mythological scenes," "circus scenes," "burlesque scenes" and "ribald scenes," mustering the same old characters—acrobats, circus riders, ballet dancers, the man with the sheep—and some new ones, such as the "musketeer painter," the "watermelon eaters" and the roguish, metamorphosable little people we find in the folklore of many regions. This mythical population engages in extremely earthy occupations. "The characters," writes Michel Leiris, "appear sometimes singly, sometimes in pairs (occasionally, it would seem, for love's sake: about to make it, in the act of making it, or just having made it)." Here a too young Daphnis gazes at a Chloe who is lost in thought; there pipe-playing fauns surprise her in a thicket (where she has, quite literally, brought her pillow); there again we assist at an embrace that needs no commentary.

Recumbent nudes, painters' studios, amorous Minotaurs, harassed nymphs and Bacchic scenes also featured in Picasso's earlier works. Was that eroticism? The answer must be Yes if one takes that word to mean the assertion of Eros without dramatic effects. No, if one thinks of the cerebral transpositions of "The Bride stripped bare by her Bachelors." It would be equally fruitless to seek the "transgression" dear to Georges Bataille. Whether it is a matter of light-weight variations on the theme of furtiveness and clandestinity—the ribbons and laces, the peeps at girls on swings or through half-open doors, in which eighteenth-century libertines delighted—or of ritualistic arrangements involving all the weaponry of terror dear to the Marquis de Sade, it would seem that eroticism only exists where there is prohibition and transgression, whether ingenious or perverse. Here prohibition vanishes in a guiltless world. Should one speak of eroticism or rather of innocent sexuality?

Picasso says that "it is only when painting is not painting that there can be any question of outrage." Adequate detachment is ensured by a handwriting of unprecedented sincerity, even for Picasso, where all corrections and emphases have been retained *without exception*: simultaneous versions of a profile, a pencil that lingers on a line or a head of hair, spontaneous brushwork that gives the plastic art most favorable to pretences the appearance of candor. This is a new manifestation of Picassian irony: the imprescriptible right to smile is asserted in opposition to the gravity and stereotyped tedium of a "planetary art." Midway between pure drawing and literature, these little poems in prose seem made expressly to drive monolithic purists to despair. Needless to say, the antiquarian fiction aims less at "killing modern art" than at covering nostalgia with a transparent veil. As during the Harlequin period, the most worn-out mask becomes the most delicate pretext, for these confessions are not devoid of a certain ambiguity. Perhaps an art that knows neither tragedy nor joy never disclosed its mock gravity more clearly than in this ironical salute to ancient Beauty, this smiling dream of Desire as the fleeting image of Happiness.

ETCHING, MARCH 16-22, 1968.

This is one of the 347 prints Picasso did in 1968 and showed in Paris in December of that year. It is an etching and took several days to finish. Against a background filled with faces we see the artist contemplating some of the familiar characters of his world: the generously proportioned Circus Rider mounted on a genuine stallion, a sleeping Man in the center and, facing the painter, his mythical double, the Sculptor demigod, the bearded Man frequently met with in Picasso's earlier engravings, balanced on the left by an austere Iberian profile.

PICASSO AND CULTURE

Man could not repeat himself even if he wanted
to. To repeat is to transgress the law of the
spirit, its flight forwards.

PICASSO

"THIS œuvre, whose roots thrust down into the last century,
through its historical situation and the very long period it
covers with the most constant exuberance, and through the
half-playful, half-dramatic element that is uniquely its own,
remains alive and young, as is also proved by the discussions
it still stirs up" (André Breton). Of all its aspects none is more
topical or more singular than its ambivalent relation to culture.

In this art two aesthetics labeled "Ingrism" and "Cubism"
confront each other. It is not so much the opposition of past
and present, but rather of the poetry of reminiscence to the
poetry of rupture. The first assembles the most volatile products
of the image-makers of the past, the most exquisite essences of
our cultural heritage. Evoking the Circus, the Dance, the Fable,
the Theater, it offers us the spectacle of a spectacle. The second
breaks away from all theatrical performance.

But the opposition between the two is not absolute, for
reminiscence is not pastiche. Unlike the palinodes of a Dali who
exalts Meissonier or a Chirico in his latest phase, both of whom
receive the approval of certain critics, Picasso's Ingrism does
not involve the slightest retractation. His recent works are proof
of that: the melody of the past comes to life again solely in the
shape of nostalgia. It is creation at one remove and in inverted
commas, proposed in a context of allusion or imperceptible
irony—literature. "Oh!" said Picasso one day, "that is my
Sunday painting."

The Cubist aesthetic, instead, implies the total rejection of all that Pierre Charpentrat, speaking of the French taste in architecture, termed "sentimental historicity." But Cubism underwent the usual treatment: the operation that had raised it to the rank of a taboo reduced it treacherously to a simple cultural vicissitude. By virtue of the cautious eclecticism that in recent decades has made criticism the antechamber of history, the first art that broke openly with Culture has been simply brought back into the cultural fold. This involved forgetting that, after the phases of Cézannesque and analytic transition, Cubism was actually a sort of Pop art. As Dubuffet wrote not long ago, "western man's idea that culture is a question of books, paintings and monuments is childish . . . But in this context I use the word culture in a sense—the sense of development and refinement of intellectual activity—which is not the one usually endorsed by our school-teachers." And he went on to compare our "classifying" and "fixing" culture with "the only salutary regime for artistic creation: permanent revolution." If one is willing to ignore the boisterous topicality that term suggests today, there could be no better definition of Picasso's project.

"Pictures are always begotten the way princes beget their children: with shepherdesses. You never paint the Parthenon . . . You make pictures with a little shack in the South, a packet of tobacco, or an old chair." Rags and scraps of paper, bits of trash, childish daubs, and studied techniques pitilessly simplified, reveal the unity in diversity of the "refined brutalism" which by historical accident earned the name of Cubism.

Where other painters merely substituted the cult of the packet of tobacco for that of the Parthenon, Picasso replaced the traditional languages of Painting with a "half-dramatic, half-playful" poetry in which fantasy itself is assumed with a certain obstinacy. This taking possession of the world, alternately subtle and violent, sometimes delights in extracting the most refined concretions from the strata of the past, sometimes bursts asunder the straitjacket of imitation. How can the fragile tissue of words express all this without misinterpreting it? Who would think of translating a poem by Eluard into the language used in the days of Anatole France? Picasso is well aware of this hiatus. "What we need," he told Christian Zervos in 1935, "is a dictatorship of painters" to eliminate "cheats, habits, charm, history." The use of the literary language of tradition may be justified in connection with Picasso's committed painting, his Ingresque or anecdotic works and his reminiscences of the Image; but where there is a question of the "broken" figuration that relates, however distantly, to the Cubist aesthetic or of the new poetic objects that persist paradoxically in making signs to the world, how else can one describe them than in their own plastic entity? They escape the limits of language, for in the last analysis all non-poetic language is merely a combination of already known meanings. And the artist, like the scholar, is always on the look-out for the other meaning, for what Lévi-Strauss calls "the other message."

"I walked down the rue Saint-Denis the other day," Picasso related in 1952. "It's wonderful ... The prostitutes lined up on the sidewalks, the costermongers, the flowers. I said to myself: 'Of course, a glass and a packet of cigarettes, that's beautiful and just as difficult to paint as the Last Judgment, but it would be splendid if one could paint that—the life of a big city.'"

It's not that Picasso is homesick for the Subject, but no creative artist is willing to sacrifice definitively the sparkling anarchy of life to the immutable order of a language. He prefers the subversion of a poem to the heritage of a culture. That is why, on the cypress-crowned hill that lies opposite Mougins and looks down on the Mediterranean in the distance, Picasso still works just as furiously as ever.

SELECT BIBLIOGRAPHY
CHIEF EXHIBITIONS
GENERAL INDEX
LIST OF ILLUSTRATIONS
TABLE OF CONTENTS

SELECT BIBLIOGRAPHY

The standard catalogue of Picasso's work, edited by Christian ZERVOS, has been published at intervals by Cahiers d'Art, Paris, since 1932 and at present numbers twenty volumes:

Oeuvres de 1895 à 1906, 1932 (reprinted 1957). — *Oeuvres de 1906 à 1912* and *Oeuvres de 1912 à 1917* (in two volumes), 1942. — *Oeuvres de 1917 à 1919*, 1949. — *Oeuvres de 1920 à 1922*, 1951. — *Oeuvres de 1923 à 1925*, 1952. — Supplement to Volumes I-V, 1952. — *Oeuvres de 1926 à 1932*, 1955. — *Oeuvres de 1932 à 1937*, 1957. — *Oeuvres de 1937 à 1939*, 1959. — *Oeuvres de 1939 et 1940*, 1959. — *Oeuvres de 1940 et 1941*, 1960. — *Oeuvres de 1942 et 1943*, 1961. — *Oeuvres de 1943 et 1944*, 1962. — *Oeuvres de 1944 à 1946*, 1963. — *Oeuvres de 1946 à 1953*, 1965. — *Oeuvres de 1953 à 1955*, 1965. — *Oeuvres de 1956 et 1957*, 1966. — *Oeuvres de 1958 et 1959*, 1967. — *Oeuvres de 1959 à 1961*, 1968. — *Oeuvres de 1961 et 1962*, 1968.

★

The first volume devoted to Picasso in the Taste of Our Time series (Skira, Geneva 1953), written by Maurice RAYNAL, contained a select bibliography up to about 1950. The following bibliography covers books and articles published from 1950 on:

Memoirs and Intimate Records

A. SALMON, *Souvenirs sans fin*, Paris 1955-1956. — H. PARMELIN, *Picasso sur la place*, Paris 1960. — BRASSAÏ, *Conversations avec Picasso*, Paris 1964.

Monographs and Works on Special Aspects of Picasso

A. CIRICI-PELLICER, *Picasso avant Picasso*, Geneva 1950 (Spanish edition, Barcelona 1946). — J. LASSAIGNE, *Picasso*, Paris 1950. — M. GIEURE, *Initiation à l'œuvre de Picasso*, Paris 1951. — A. VERDET, *Pablo Picasso au Musée d'Antibes*, Paris 1951. — G. SCHMIDT, *Pablo Picasso*, Basel 1952. — E. ROSENTHAL, *Picasso, Painter and Engraver*, San Francisco 1952. — W. S. LIEBERMAN, *Picasso: Blue and Rose Periods*, New York 1952. — T. TZARA,

Picasso et la poésie, Rome 1953. — C. ROY, *Picasso, La Guerre et La Paix*, Paris 1953. — G. C. ARGAN, *Scultura di Picasso*, Venice 1953. — J. SABARTÈS, *Picasso ceramista*, Milan 1953. — F. OLIVIER, *Picasso*, Paris 1954. —F. RUSSOLI, *Pablo Picasso*, Milan and Paris 1954. — J. SABARTÈS, *Picasso, documents iconographiques*, Geneva 1954. — W. BOECK and J. SABARTÈS, *Picasso*, London 1955. — F. ELGAR and R. MAILLARD, *Picasso*, London 1955. — VERCORS, *Picasso, Oeuvres des musées de Leningrad et Moscou*, Paris 1955. — B. GEISER, *Picasso, peintre-graveur*, Bern 1955. — B. GEISER and H. BOLLIGER, *L'oeuvre gravé de Picasso*, Lausanne 1955 (in English, New York and London 1955). — M. JARDOT, *Picasso 1900-1955*, Munich 1956. — P. DESCARGUES, *Picasso, témoin du XXe siècle*, Paris 1956. — J. CAMON AZNAR, *Picasso y el cubismo*, Barcelona 1956. — A. VALENTIN, *Picasso*, Paris 1957. — R. PENROSE, *Portrait of Picasso*, New York 1957. — D. D. DUNCAN, *The Private World of Pablo Picasso*, New York 1958. — R. PENROSE, *Picasso, His Life and Work*, London 1958. — J. SABARTÈS, *Les Ménines*, Paris and London 1958. — L. GUNTHER, *Picasso: A Pictorial Biography*, New York 1959. — L. G. BUCHHEIM, *Picasso*, London 1959. — M. JARDOT, *Picasso (dessins)*, Paris 1959. — J. PRÉVERT, *Portraits de Picasso*, Milan 1959. — P. de CHAMPRIS, *Picasso, ombre et soleil*, Paris 1960. — G. DIEHL, *Picasso*, Paris 1960. — DOR DE LA SOUCHÈRE, *Picasso à Antibes*, Paris 1960 (English edition, London 1960). — L. M. DOMINGUIN and G. BOUDAILLE, *Toros y toreros*, Paris 1961 (in English, New York and London 1961). — D. D. DUNCAN, *Picasso's Picassos*, New York and London 1961. — R. ARNHEIM, *Picasso's Guernica, The Genesis of a Painting*, Los Angeles 1962. — A. BLUNT and P. POOL, *Picasso, The Formative Years*, London 1962. — D. COOPER, *Picasso, Les Déjeuners*, New York and London 1963. — F. GILOT and C. LAKE, *Life with Picasso*, New York 1964. — J. K. FOSTER, *Posters of Picasso*, New York 1964. — F. MOURLOT, *Picasso lithographe, 1919-1963*, 4 volumes, Monte Carlo 1949-1964. — P. DAIX, introduction by J. SABARTÈS, *Picasso*, Paris 1964 (English edition, London 1965). — J. RICHARDSON, *Picasso, Watercolours and Gouaches*, London 1964. — H. BERGGRUEN, *Picasso, 60 ans de gravure*, Paris 1964. — H. JAFFÉ, *Picasso*, New York 1964. — M. DE MICHELI, *Scritti di Picasso*, Milan 1964. — S. TAKASHINA, *Picasso*, Tokyo 1964. — G. BOUDAILLE, *Picasso, première époque, 1881-1906*, Paris 1964. — H. PARMELIN, *Les Dames de Mougins*, Paris 1964. — J. BERGER, *Success and Failure of Picasso*, London 1965. — H. KAY, *Picasso, le monde des enfants*, Grenoble 1965. — H. PARMELIN, *Le peintre et son modèle*, Paris 1965. — E. QUINN and R. PENROSE, *Picasso at Work*, New York and London 1965. — P. GASCAR, G. PATRIX, M. RAGON, *Picasso et le béton*, Paris n.d. (1965). — P. DAIX and G. BOUDAILLE, *Picasso 1900-1906*, Neuchâtel-Paris 1966. — H. PARMELIN, *Notre-Dame-de-Vie*, Paris 1966. — K. LEONHARD and H. BOLLIGER, *L'oeuvre gravé de Picasso*, Lausanne 1966 (in English, New York and London 1966). — R. PENROSE, *The Sculpture of Picasso*, New York 1967. — D. COOPER, *Picasso: Theatre*, London 1967. — A. FERMIGIER, M. del CASTILLO, J. GRENIER,

P. Guinard, D. Milhau, G. Picon, C. Roy, D. Vallier, *Picasso*, Paris 1967. — J. Leymarie, *Picasso Drawings*, Geneva 1967. — C. Czwiklitzer, *290 Affiches de Pablo Picasso*, published by the author, 1968.

Special Issues and Magazine Articles

Verve, VII, No. 25-26, Paris 1951. — Le Point, XLII, Souillac, October 1952. — Commentari, IV, No. 3, Rome 1953. — La Biennale di Venezia, No. 13-14, Venice 1953. — Realismo, Rome, March-April 1953. — Du, No. 7, Zurich, July 1954. — Verve, VIII, No. 29-30, Paris 1954. — L'Oeil, No. 4, Paris 1955 (article by R. Bernier, *Barcelone, 48 Paseo de Gracia*, pp. 5-13). — Kunstwerk, IX, No. 3, 1955. — The Burlington Magazine, June 1957 (article by J. Richardson, *Picasso's Ateliers and Other Recent Works*, pp. 183-193). — The Burlington Magazine, May 1958 (article by J. Golding, *The Demoiselles d'Avignon*, pp. 155-163). — Papeles de son Armadans, V, No. 49, Valencia 1960. — L'Oeil, Paris, October 1961 (article by L. Prejger, *Picasso découpe le fer*, pp. 28-33). — La Nouvelle Critique, No. 30, Paris, November 1961. — España Libre, 1965 (article by G. C. Argan, *Picasso, il simbolo e il mito*). — The Burlington Magazine, January 1966 (article by J. S. Boggs, *Picasso and the Theatre at Toulouse*, p. 53).

Illustrated Books

A. Césaire, *Corps perdu*, Paris 1950 (32 engravings). — T. Tzara, *De mémoire d'homme*, Paris 1950 (9 lithographs). — P. Eluard, *Le visage de la Paix*, Paris 1951 (29 drawings). — A. de Monluc, *La maigre*, Paris 1952 (10 drypoints). — M. Toesca, *Six contes fantasques*, Paris 1953 (6 copper engravings). — P. Picasso, *Poèmes et lithographies*, Paris 1954 (14 lithographs). — T. Tzara, *A haute flamme*, Paris 1955 (6 etchings). — Roch Grey, *Chevaux de minuit, Epopée*, Paris 1956 (13 drypoints and copper engravings). — M. Jacob, *Chronique des temps héroïques*, Paris 1956 (3 drypoints, 3 lithographs). — José Delgado (alias Pepe Illo), *La Tauromaquia, O arte de torear*, Barcelona 1959 (26 aquatints and one etching). — P. Picasso, *Le frère mendiant* or *Libro del Conocimiento*, Paris 1959 (18 drypoints). — P. Neruda, *Toros*, Paris 1960 (15 wash drawings). — J. Sabartés, *A los toros avec Picasso*, Paris 1961 (103 wash drawings, 4 lithographs).

Stage Sets

Chant funèbre pour Ignacio Sanchez Mejias, by Garcia Lorca (choreography by Lupovici), Paris 1953. — *Icare*, ballet by Serge Lifar, Paris 1962.

CHIEF EXHIBITIONS

1949, Paris, Maison de la Pensée Française (works 1945-1949). — 1950, London, Arts Council of Great Britain, *Picasso in Provence*. — 1950-1951, Paris, Maison de la Pensée Française (sculptures and drawings, text by L. ARAGON). — 1951, Basel, Berlin, Essen, Freiburg-im-Breisgau, Hamburg, Munich, Nuremberg, Stuttgart, *Etchings and Lithographs 1905-1951* (preface by L. GROTE, text by D. H. KAHNWEILER). — 1953, Lyons, Musée des Beaux-Arts. — 1953, Rome, Galleria Nazionale d'Arte Moderna (introduction by L. VENTURI). — 1953, Milan, Palazzo Reale (introduction by F. RUSSOLI). — 1953, Amsterdam, Stedelijk Museum (lithographs, aquatints, bronzes). — 1954, Liège, Musée des Beaux-Arts (graphic work, preface by T. TZARA). — 1954, Zurich, Kunsthaus, *The Graphic Work* (preface by R. WEHRLI, introduction by B. GEISER, catalogue by H. BOLLIGER). — 1954, São Paulo, Museu de Arte moderna. — 1954, Paris, Maison de la Pensée Française, *Picasso, Two Periods, 1900-1914 and 1950-1954*. — 1954, Paris, Galerie Berggruen, *Picasso, Drawings 1903-1907* (introduction by D. H. KAHNWEILER). — 1955, Paris, Musée des Arts décoratifs (catalogue by M. JARDOT). — 1955, Paris, Bibliothèque Nationale, *The Graphic Work*. — 1955, Munich, Haus der Kunst, *Picasso 1900-1955* (introduction by M. JARDOT). — 1955, London, Marlborough Gallery (drawings and bronzes). — 1956, Cologne, Rheinisches Museum and Hamburg, Kunsthalle. — 1956, Malmö, Museum, *Homage to Picasso, Bergengren Collection*. — 1956, Geneva, Musée d'Art et d'Histoire, *Picasso, Nonell, Manolo*. — 1956, Paris, Galerie Berggruen, *Picasso, Drawings of Half a Century* (preface by M. JARDOT). — 1957, Paris, Galerie Louise Leiris, *Paintings 1955-1956* (preface by D. H. KAHNWEILER). — 1957, New York, Museum of Modern Art and Chicago, Art Institute. — 1958, Paris, Maison de la Pensée Française, *150 Original Ceramics* (texts by G. and S. RAMIÉ and H. PARMELIN). — 1958, Philadelphia Museum of Art (preface by Henry CLIFFORD). — 1959, Marseilles, Musée Cantini (introduction by D. COOPER). — 1959, Paris, Galerie Louise Leiris, *Les Ménines, 1957*. — 1960, London, Tate Gallery (introduction by R. PENROSE). — 1960, Paris, Bibliothèque Nationale, *Engravings* (introduction by J. ADHÉMAR). — 1960, Paris, Galerie Louise Leiris (45 linocuts 1958-1960, and drawings 1959-1960). — 1960, Faenza, Museo Internazionale delle Ceramiche (42 ceramics). — 1961, Los Angeles, University of California Art Gallery. — 1961, Lucerne, Galerie Rosengart (paintings 1950-1960). — 1962, New York, *Picasso: An American Tribute.* — 1962, London, Marlborough Gallery, *Picasso, Important Paintings, Watercolours, and New Linocuts* (with Henry Moore and other 20th-century artists). — 1962, Paris, Galerie Louise Leiris, *Paintings, Vauvenargues 1959-1961* and *Le Déjeuner sur l'herbe 1960-1961.* — 1963, Lucerne, Galerie Rosengart (paintings 1912-1927 and 1952-1961). — 1964, Montreal Museum of Fine Arts and Toronto Art Gallery (catalogue by J. S. BOGGS). — 1964, Tokyo, Kyoto, Nagoya. — 1964, Paris, Galerie Louise Leiris, *Paintings 1962-1963.* — 1964, Paris, Galerie Berggruen, *Picasso, 60 Years of Engraving.* — 1964, Zurich and London, Gimpel Gallery, and Hanover, *Paintings 1945-1961.* — 1965, Toulouse, Musée des Augustins, *Picasso and the Theater.* — 1965, New York, Perls Galleries. — 1966, Tel Aviv, Helena Rubenstein Pavilion. — 1966, Los Angeles County Museum, *Picasso, Sixty Years of Graphic Works.* — Washington, Gallery of Modern Art, *Picasso since 1945.* — 1966, Lucerne, Galerie Rosengart (paintings 1960-1965). — 1966-1967, Paris, Grand and Petit Palais, *Homage to Picasso* (paintings, drawings, sculptures, ceramics, catalogue by J. LEYMARIE). — 1967, Amsterdam, Stedelijk Museum. — 1967, London, Tate Gallery (sculptures, ceramics, graphic works, introduction by R. PENROSE). — 1967, New York, Museum of Modern Art (sculptures, constructions, ceramics, etc., introduction by M. WHEELER and R. PENROSE). — 1967, Fort Worth Art Center Museum and Dallas Museum of Fine Arts (introduction by D. COOPER). — 1968, Paris, Galerie Louise Leiris, *Drawings 1966-1967* and *347 Recent Engravings.* — 1968, Baden Baden, Staatliche Kunsthalle, *Pablo Picasso, The Late Work.* — 1968, Dortmund, Museum am Ostwald.

GENERAL INDEX

LIST OF ILLUSTRATIONS

137

CONTENTS

THIS, THE FORTY-NINTH VOLUME OF THE COLLECTION "THE
TASTE OF OUR TIME," WAS PRODUCED BY THE TECHNICAL STAFF
OF EDITIONS D'ART ALBERT SKIRA. FINISHED THE FIFTEENTH
DAY OF MARCH NINETEEN HUNDRED AND SIXTY-NINE.

TEXT AND COLOR PLATES PRINTED BY

COLOR STUDIOS
AT IMPRIMERIES RÉUNIES S.A., LAUSANNE

PLATES ENGRAVED BY
GUEZELLE & RENOUARD, PARIS

BLACK AND WHITE ILLUSTRATIONS
PRINTED BY OFFSET DEPARTMENT
IMPRIMERIES RÉUNIES S.A., LAUSANNE

PHOTOGRAPHS BY

*Maurice Babey, Basel (pages 3, 22, 23, 37, 38, 43, 62, 68, 69, 74, 87, 98, 104),
Geoffrey Clements Inc., New York (pages 82, 89, 100 and front of dustjacket),
John R. Freeman Ltd., London (page 31), Mats Holmstrand, Kristinehamn,
Sweden (page 111), Walter Kirchberger, Dortmund (page 101), Henri Mardyks,
Puteaux, France (pages 24, 45, 53, 64, 78, 80), MAS, Barcelona (pages 84, 86,
90, 91), Dr Salchow, Cologne (page 63), and by courtesy of the Museum of Fine
Arts, Boston (page 96), the Art Institute of Chicago (page 70), the Museum of
Modern Art, New York (page 32), Perls Galleries, New York (page 81), Galerie
Louise Leiris, Paris (pages 28, 40, 42, 44, 46, 47, 50, 54, 56, 58, 59, 105, 108, 114,
115, 118), J. E. Bulloz, Paris (pages 88, 92), Draeger Frères Imprimeurs, Montrouge,
Paris (pages 72, 93), Unesco, Paris, Jacqueline Hyde and Eileen Tweedy, photo-
graphers (back of dustjacket). The illustration on page 60 comes from the magazine
Verve, No. 29-30, Paris 1954.*

PRINTED IN SWITZERLAND